RELEASED

College Testing

A Guide to Practices and Programs

COMMITTEE ON MEASUREMENT AND EVALUATION

Appointed by the American Council on Education

PAUL R. ANDERSON, President, Chatham College, *Chairman*

BESSIE B. COLLINS, Dean of Women, University of Delaware

SIDNEY J. FRENCH, Dean, Rollins College

HOWARD B. JEFFERSON, President, Clark University

E. F. LINDQUIST, Professor of Education, State University of Iowa

VERY REV. M. J. MCKEOUGH, O.P., Dean, St. Norbert College

C. ROBERT PACE, Director, Evaluation Service Center, Syracuse University

PAUL T. RANKIN, Assistant Superintendent, Michigan Board of Education

JAMES REYNOLDS, Professor of Junior College Education, University of Texas

W. HUGH STICKLER, Director, Office of Educational Research and Service, Florida State University

WILLIAM W. TURNBULL, Executive Vice-President, Educational Testing Service

RALPH W. TYLER, Director, Center for Advanced Study in the Behavorial Sciences, Stanford, California

ARTHUR S. ADAMS, President, American Council on Education, *ex officio*

FRANK C. ABBOTT, Secretary

COLLEGE TESTING

A GUIDE TO
PRACTICES AND PROGRAMS

PREPARED BY THE COMMITTEE ON
MEASUREMENT AND EVALUATION OF THE
AMERICAN COUNCIL ON EDUCATION

AMERICAN COUNCIL ON EDUCATION
Washington, D.C.

Foreword

IN THE APPRAISAL OF INTELLECTUAL QUALITIES AND ATTAINMENTS, tests have a contribution to make that may seem self-evident today, when formal testing procedures are being widely used in the elementary and secondary schools, at the point of admission to college, in placement within the college program, in appraising individual and group achievement in college, at the point of entry into graduate and professional schools, in conjunction with entry into professional practice, and in many other ways.

Indeed, in the judgment of the members of the Committee on Measurement and Evaluation, a major contemporary problem in education is that the American public—on and off the college campus—seems too ready to assume that test procedures and test results can provide complete and final answers to the many serious problems of evaluation that we face.

To the extent that testing helps to focus attention on the individual in our educational processes, we can all applaud. But whether individuals are really helped or harmed will depend on the ways in which tests are used and interpreted. In a day in which testing is applied from the cradle to the grave, it is of crucial importance that those who use the tests understand what they can and do show and what they cannot and do not show.

This book has been prepared for the college teacher and administrator who is now concerned—and likely to be more so—with testing procedures and materials but who is without formal training in the techniques of testing. The Committee on Measurement and Evaluation hopes that it will assist teachers and administrators alike to put tests to use in ways that are appropriate and that contribute to their efforts to keep the individual student at the center of the stage in all of his own uniqueness.

Many individuals have aided in the preparation of this book, as the chairman of the committee, Paul R. Anderson, has pointed out in his Preface. The Educational Testing Service encouraged and aided the project in important ways; the W. T. Grant Foundation supplied funds which helped make publication possible. To all of these, the committee and the Council are grateful.

ARTHUR S. ADAMS, *President*
American Council on Education

Preface

THE USE OF MEASUREMENT DEVICES IN INSTITUTIONS OF HIGHER learning has increased by leaps and bounds since the war, partly stimulated by the widespread development and use of tests by the military services in the early 1940's. Expanding enrollments in the 1960's will in all likelihood result in further extension of this practice.

The refinement of evaluation instruments has developed more rapidly than the sophistication of the consumer. Graduate programs, with few exceptions, fail to provide training in the arts and techniques of effective instruction. The result is that all too many professors and administrators possess little or no understanding of tests, their applicability, their range of utility, or their limitations. Lack of knowledge rather than of interest accounts both for failure to take advantage of many splendid instruments currently available and also for some misuse of them.

This situation stimulated the Committee on Measurement and Evaluation of the American Council on Education to consider the advisability of preparing a manual for teachers and others not expert in testing covering the principal characteristics and uses of tests in various areas such as admissions, placement, and instruction. The present volume is the result. Its purpose is to serve not the specialist in the field but a large group of people in higher education who would like to make greater use of evaluation instruments and yet who know relatively little about either their potential or their limitations. This guide should provide such a person with a background of knowledge in the field and lead him to references through which he can carry his inquiry as far as he likes.

The project was administered under an editorial subcommittee composed of E. F. Lindquist, C. Robert Pace, Ralph W. Tyler, and the writer working cooperatively with staff members of the Educational Testing Services ably marshaled by Anna Dragositz. Ideas and initial drafts were provided by William E. Coffman, Anna

vii

Dragositz, John S. Helmick, A. Pemberton Johnson, Gerald V. Lannholm, Richard Pearson, and Barbara Wagner. In order to provide unity of style and an approach to the material based upon campus experience and possible use, Lily Detchen, director of evaluation services at Chatham College, did the final editing. *College Testing: A Guide to Practices and Programs* is thus a product of a number of minds and we hope the better for being so.

From the beginning it was felt that a practical guide should include representative examples of programs in action. Part II of the volume is composed of descriptive articles by persons intimately involved in the programs in seven institutions. In contrast to Part I, which the Committee on Measurement and Evaluation has studied and approved, Part II is the product of individual authors.

The Committee on Measurement and Evaluation acknowledges with deep appreciation the contribution which the various planners, authors, and editors have made. Without their deep interest in the project and their uncommon willingness to have their own contributions reviewed, revised, and rewritten in line with committee desire, this volume could never have been possible.

It is the committee's hope that readers will find here materials helpful to the resolution of teaching and other educational problems in their own institutions and that this volume may therefore serve a useful purpose in the improvement of higher education.

PAUL R. ANDERSON, *Chairman*
Committee on Measurement and Evaluation

Contents

ix

PART I

The Role of Measurement in Relation
to Educational Problems of the College

I. The Status and Basic Purposes of College Testing

THE USE OF TESTS AT THE COLLEGE LEVEL HAS INCREASED PHENOME-
nally in recent years and foreseeable pressures indicate an even
greater need of tests in the future. Increases in the college-age population, improvement in the socioeconomic status of American
families, trends in the general economy that encourage young
people to remain in school, the ever-growing conviction that more
of our high school graduates are entitled to a higher education,
and the need of our nation for college-educated people—all these
are factors in the greater activity in testing. One major college
admissions testing agency reports that its activities increased by
more than 500 percent in a recent eight-year period, and more
recently increased by 50 percent from one year to the next. State
testing programs have seen rapid growth in twenty-six states,
usually at the twelfth-grade level, although the trend is toward
beginning testing at earlier levels. Other states have similar programs under consideration.

In addition to the admissions and placement tests so widely used,
many other kinds of tests have been developed for additional educational purposes. Such interest has emerged from a widespread
effort in higher education to rethink the objectives of institutional
curricula and services. This has frequently resulted in the introduction of programs of general education, in improving the selection of students for professional and other specialized programs,
and in general in a greater consideration of the students as individuals. In the course of instituting changes, a need evolved for
evaluating the result of such changes, hence the development of
tests for special purposes.

Interest in the theory and methodology of testing at the college
level was given great impetus by the Thurstones at the University
of Chicago in the early twenties when they introduced "psycho-

3

logical aptitude" testing, and a little later developed the American Council on Education Psychological Examination for College Freshmen, which was first used as a selective admissions test at the University of Chicago and subsequently adopted by hundreds of other higher institutions. The ACE Psychological Examination had followed rapidly the success of group intelligence testing in the United States Army in World War I which had helped solve some of the selection problems for specialized branches of the military service. Dr. L. L. Thurstone was the author of many of the tests used in World War I. His interest continued unabated in the peacetime interim between world wars and he inspired and stimulated much of the work of others which improved both scholastic aptitude and achievement measures. The individual student rather than the group became the focus of testing. In aptitude testing, the concept of special or "differential" aptitudes was developed; and in achievement testing, diagnostic measures for ascertaining the strengths and weaknesses of the individual, testing for the achievement of specific objectives of instruction rather than for mastery of a rather vague "general" content, and the improvement of norms from the standpoint of closer descriptions of student groups were stressed.

The advent of World War II stressed the vital need for identifying men and women best suited to specialized tasks and created an upsurge of interest and much progress in testing research and the development of instruments. This relatively new science was now on firm ground and was recognized as an important technique for peacetime purposes as well as war. During the last fifteen years, several major cooperative enterprises in higher education have undertaken systematic evaluations of the outcomes of college instruction, stressing the identification of educational outcomes and providing information of assistance and importance to the classroom teacher.

The use and understanding of tests is not as complex as nonspecialists may assume. It is hoped that this book may prove that point. Many members of college staffs who are not trained professionally in college testing are called upon to use test results and need to be able to interpret them and to understand some of the uses of tests made in their institutions. Indeed, many of these persons—both teachers and administrators—would like to use tests but don't quite know how to go about it. The discussions here are designed for this group. The aim is to provide them with enough background to serve their purpose, enough description of content and method to enable them to choose the test most useful to them, enough of the technique for practical use, and enough information in general to enable them to distinguish between the tests useful to nonspecialists and those which require the closer attention of the specialist.

THE KINDS OF TESTS IN GENERAL USE

Any discussion of the status of college testing may well begin with a description of the kinds of tests and examinations that are now in fairly general use. There are several categories of these, generally designated as scholastic aptitude, achievement, interests, personal adjustment, and special abilities (or aptitudes) tests. These tests may have been developed by classroom instructors or college departmental staffs; by nonprofit research organizations or other groups representative of education; by research centers attached to universities that receive commissions to produce tests needed for particular purposes; by individuals who secure publication through commercial publishers; by publishing houses that maintain staffs for this purpose; by groups of college faculty members who cooperate under the auspices of some special project to produce tests they need in common; by boards of professional examiners attached to universities, to civil service examining units, to state departments of education and to city educational systems, and so on.

Scholastic aptitude tests

Just what academic learning ability is or whether it exists in any absolute sense is difficult to say, but the day has long since passed when measurement specialists say they are attempting to measure any unique quality called "intelligence" or any abstract psychological factors which are attributes of unique mental functions, although in the early days of measurement it was hoped that this might be possible. Experience has proved otherwise.

From the beginning of mental testing, constructors of tests have tended to avoid the bizarre and have worked on the assumption that the best way to obtain an index of relative ability to learn is to incorporate in the test problems only materials from common experience—which actually meant usually drawn from common *school* activities. The result was that these early tests predicted school success better than success in other activities which require intellectual ability. Thus, these tests might better have been termed scholastic aptitude tests than intelligence tests.

The change in name from intelligence tests to scholastic aptitude tests indicates, at the higher academic levels at least, a change in emphasis in the test content. When the problem is that of predicting academic success, consideration is given to the abilities which are requisite to academic success. For most school learning situations, these abilities are firmly based upon verbal facility and quantitative reasoning, though other abilities are required to a lesser degree.

Thus, today's aptitude tests in intellectual areas place emphasis on reading, vocabulary skills, and understanding; on arithmetic reasoning and problem-solving; and on computational skills. All of these are learned abilities, so that these tests in a certain sense are measures of proficiency. They are not, however, achievement tests in the usual sense, since they measure generalized abilities developed over a long period of time rather than the skills and understandings which are specific to a circumscribed body of knowledge.

Because commonly used scholastic aptitude tests are measures of achievement in a broad sense, one may quite naturally raise the question: *How is it known, in any given case, whether a low score is the result of insufficient native capacity for work at the college level or the result of inadequate training in the skills and abilities measured by the test?* The answer is that the score alone does not reveal which of these two factors (or others) may be operating. Other evidences of intellectual capacity, such as previous school records or outstanding accomplishment in some intellectual area— or lack of it—have to be reviewed before the individual's probable intellectual capacity can be judged.

Let us then assume that a certain student is bright enough to do work at the college level, but simply has not had the quality of instruction to prepare him for the kinds of tasks the test sets. What now? May the score be looked upon as an indication of scholastic aptitude? In a certain sense, yes. If the student is applying to a college that, on the one hand, has very high academic standards and, on the other, makes no provision for remedial work in basic skills, the chances are that the student will find the going very difficult unless he is able to compensate for his shortcomings by great additional effort. No amount of sympathetic understanding will enable him to undertake work for which he is not ready. In situations where special remedial work is offered to students who are deficient in reading or numerical skills, for example, the score may operate less effectively as an indicator of probable scholastic success.

Achievement tests

Achievement tests measure proficiency in defined areas of learning. Normally, the tests are taken after a prescribed period of study, and results are expected to indicate how well the subject has been mastered.

Currently, there are two kinds of achievement tests: tests which measure learning in specific courses such as trigonometry, Latin, American history, and so on, and general achievement tests which cut across specific course boundaries to measure learning attained in a broad field of study such as the humanities, social studies, or science. Both types might be further classified into those emphasizing *factual information* and those which measure *understanding* and the ability to apply to new situations the skills and principles learned. The latter, of course, are likely to be of greater interest at the college level.

Interests tests

Although a review of academic records and scholastic aptitude tests is useful in appraising student interests, there are certain rather obvious shortcomings in relying on them too heavily. The meaning of grades is actually obscure because so many factors are involved—native ability, the enthusiasm that teachers have engendered in students, and the subjective judgments of the graders, to name but a few. It is useful to supplement grades and scholastic aptitude tests with evidences of interests from other sources.

Among the most useful sources are interest inventories, which are designed to reveal information on an individual's predominant interest patterns. Some are intended to appraise academic interests, but the most commonly used measures are based on vocational interest patterns. Here, two general types are available: one type, of which the Strong Vocational Interest Blank is an example, is scorable in terms of specific jobs or occupations such as lawyer, engineer, minister, journalist, and so on. The other, of which the Kuder Preference Record is an example, yields scores related to broad areas of interest, such as scientific, literary, or persuasive, which, in turn, may be related by a counselor to different categories of jobs and professions.

Tests for specific occupations are generally more time-consuming and are expensive to score. If only a general idea of predominant interests is needed, a broad-area inventory may be all that is indicated. In some situations it may be useful to administer both types. Also, it should be noted that some appear to work better with younger students than others and some seem to be more useful with one sex than the other sex. The decision to use any interest inventory at all should rest primarily on whether the college has a staff member who is trained in the use and interpretation of such instruments.

Personal and social adjustment tests

Personal characteristics other than predominant interests obviously play an important role in success. And, as all will agree, it is these intangible factors that are so difficult to tie down for objective appraisal by group-administered measurement techniques.

A great deal can, of course, be learned about an individual if he undergoes a diagnostic review by a trained clinical team. Few colleges, however, could afford the service of a team of this kind for the screening of all students. The work of such specialists is directed primarily toward individuals who are coping with problems so difficult as to interfere seriously with their ability to utilize their skills, interests, and abilities effectively in day-to-day living.

Most college students do not fall into this category. They are, by and large, normal, healthy, maturing young people, and the kind of information needed is that which will reflect their personal qualities and be useful to them in making long-range personal and vocational choices.

Inventories planned to yield information of this sort are available. Unfortunately, however, a number of them have grown out of clinically oriented situations and have little meaning except to clinicians. The questionable selection and definition of aspects of personality selected for scoring is not, however, the only limitation such inventories have. A more basic limitation, even for the trained user, is a lack of data establishing the extent to which their measurements are valid.

Measurements of special abilities and aptitudes

A host of tests has been developed to measure artistic, musical, scientific, clerical, and mechanical aptitudes and other special abilities.[1] Also, there are measures of visual discrimination, verbal facility, numerical ability, memory ability, figure relations, finger and manual dexterity, and so forth. Some are presented in the familiar paper-and-pencil form of objective tests; others are performance tests which require the individual to work directly with special materials, such as might be needed to assemble a lock or to manipulate small objects quickly. Some have been developed on the basis of specific job specifications and have been standardized on employed groups. Others have grown out of attempts to isolate and measure specific abilities which might be required for success in different types of work. Some have been related to specific kinds of vocational training, principally at the secondary school level, and provide norms for such groups. But few as yet have been developed and standardized for college populations.

By and large, traditional college populations will have less use for measures of this type than will terminal-vocational programs. For either group it is best to determine first whether any of the

---

[1] Dewey B. Stuit, *et al.*, *Predicting Success in Professional Schools.* The authors discuss prediction in engineering, law, medicine, dentistry, music, agriculture, teacher training, and nursing; they review research findings and state implications for counseling under each of these major findings.

basic aptitude and skills tests are likely to do as good a job of predicting success in a special field of study as will measures of more specific abilities. There are several reasons for this. First, many courses, despite their intent to provide training for specific occupations, depend largely on lectures and reading assignments and thereby place a premium on verbal ability. Second, some measures of so-called special aptitudes duplicate to quite a large degree the kinds of materials included in measures of general scholastic aptitude. Third, those that have been developed principally for use with employed workers are not appropriate for college students, particularly when the number of students in a program is too small for developing adequate local norms. Fourth, some of them, particularly performance tests, are rather complex to administer and interpret. Colleges which, after a thoughtful review of such tests, deem it desirable to employ them in their programs, should be prepared for their lack of norms and data on validity and reliability for college students and should be prepared to undertake special studies of their effectiveness.

PURPOSES SERVED BY TESTS

If held to their basic function as tools, tests can be of immense assistance to an institution in ascertaining to what degree it is achieving the outcomes that it expects for the kinds of students that it has, the kinds of programs that it plans for them, and the procedures of instruction and guidance that it employs. More important, tests can help the individual student to a better realization of his educational objectives.

Regardless of the kinds of tests that an institution may employ, its measurement program cannot function well unless there are clear-cut definitions of the institution's goals and educational objectives. Objectives are dictated by the philosophy of the institution, and the process of defining goals is most complex, but the importance of this first step cannot be overemphasized.[2] Only then

[2] For an informative account of how some cooperating college faculties pursued the problem of defining institutional objectives, see the report by Paul L. Dressel and Lewis Mayhew, *General Education: Explorations in Evaluation* (1954) and a similar earlier work published by the American Council on Education, *Cooperation in General Education: A Final Report of the Executive Committee on the Cooperative Study in General Education* (1947).

can tests be used to appraise the measure of achievement of those goals.

Tests aid the administrator

An effective testing program can serve the administration of a college in meeting many of its responsibilities. To suggest but a few: test results can help find the answers to such questions as: Do the current offerings fulfill the academic aims of the institution? Does the institution tend to emphasize some of its aspects to the detriment of others? Is the student body suitable for the kind of program that is offered, and vice versa? Are scholarship funds being most wisely dispensed? Tests rarely, if ever, supply exact answers to such questions, but they help to focus attention on particular issues and provide descriptive data. In a well-conceived program, the interpretation of test data contributes to understanding what is needed for the solution of the problem. The use of tests in general institutional evaluation is the subject of chapter 6.

Tests aid the instructional staff

Since faculty members are vitally involved in the achievements of their institution, they need answers to many of the same kinds of questions that press the administrators. Their interests, however, have a narrower focus, for their concern with over-all achievement is likely to be more closely related to their personal objectives in instruction.

When faculty members understand how to appraise results of tests and testing programs, they can use the information in a variety of ways. Many an instructor has simplified his problems by instituting homogeneous groupings in his classes—groupings made possible by analysis of results of tests of student aptitude, achievement, or skills. Again, instructors, being generally highly sensitive and moral individuals who are concerned that their grading practices be fair, are interested in perfecting their evaluation procedures. The faculty member assigned to a committee working on some institutional problem—for example, the determination of criteria for selective admission of students to specialized fields, say in engineering and education—can find test data highly revealing. The instructor who wishes to determine the effects of a given educational device—say, the effect on attitudes of an educational film on race relations as compared with a lecture on the subject—will find that test results will supplement and perhaps modify his subjective impressions.

Some experienced instructors maintain that the kind of test used influences dramatically the emphasis that a student gives to his study. A whole department can be revitalized by the use of special "major" examinations with students trained in the department: if the examinations are constructed by the faculty members or even by a board at the institution, teaching objectives are sharpened in the process; if the tests are externally prepared, the instructors may have either the reassurance of good results or may be challenged by the inadequate performance of their students to re-examine their materials or approach.

Important as all the foregoing outcomes of testing may be to the individual instructor, the greatest value appears when he is stimulated, in the process of constructing tests or examining test results, to re-examine the validity of his own teaching objectives, the degree to which he achieves his aims, and the appropriateness of his instructional materials, and then to revise his aims and methods accordingly.[3] This subject is given further consideration in chapter 4.

Tests aid the student

Because improved programs and methods contribute to the educational welfare of the student, some of the ways in which tests help him are implicit in the foregoing discussion. But there are more direct benefits. First of all, tests may deter him from embarking upon a program which he would be unlikely to complete successfully, or—to his life-long advantage—direct him to a program in which he can succeed. Or, early in his college career, they may identify certain underdeveloped skills which interfere with

[3] For further discussions of the use of tests in instruction, the reader is again referred to Dressel and Mayhew, *op. cit.*, and to the discussions by Walter W. Cook, Ralph W. Tyler, John G. Darley and Gordon V. Anderson, and Henry Chauncey and Norman Frederiksen, Part I, "The Functions of Measurement in Education," in E. F. Lindquist (ed.), *Educational Measurement* (1950), pp. 3–116.

his progress: the results of a diagnostic reading test or an inventory of study habits and accompanying counseling interviews are first steps toward remedying a shortcoming.

In course studies, if the student is led to expect tests which are challenging, they can stimulate his interest in the subject and cause him to improve both his study habits and methods of preparation. Or tests may obviate his having to repeat work that he has already mastered and enable him to go on to more challenging studies. On a different level the student who is unsure of himself in a subject may gain some sense of security and attainment if he finds that he has reached or exceeded the average successful performance of the large sample of students on the test.

At the decision points of a college student's career—especially at the end of the sophomore and senior years—tests can guide him to his next step, perhaps to a choice of his major study, to a decision to try for a graduate fellowship, or even to the logical decision to discontinue academic education if his progress has been unpromising. There are all kinds of tests available in a well-equipped counseling center that can help the student understand himself and help others understand him so that he may derive the optimum benefit from his higher educational experience.

The remainder of Part I is devoted to a more detailed discussion of particular aspects of formulating and using a comprehensive testing program—admissions, placement, instruction, counseling, general institutional evaluation, and, finally, the organization and administration of the institutional testing program.

In order to demonstrate the many approaches to the use of tests in improving higher education and their versatility in different situations and for different purposes, a small number of institutions were invited to tell the stories of their testing programs. These institutions were chosen as representative of various emphases in testing and various degrees of complexity of organization. Their reports appear in Part II.

2. The Use of Tests in the Admission of Students to College

NOT ALL INSTITUTIONS HAVE PROBLEMS OF STUDENT SELECTION, SINCE many are required by law or purpose to admit all applicants who are high school graduates—and adults who are not; such institutions can only strive to provide the array of curricula needed to fit a heterogeneous student body and perhaps later eliminate those who are not suited to the curricular offerings. While such institutions may well take advantage of preadmissions testing to improve student placement and guidance, these are not purposes related to selective admissions and so will not be treated here.

FACTORS RELATING TO THE LOCAL SITUATION

There are, however, institutions where enrollment must be limited, sometimes because of the special kind of education deemed appropriate for students of specific talents or interests, or, frequently, by reason of what is considered suitable institutional size in terms of aims, geographic location, and plant. For the latter institutions, the information that tests provide both systematically and objectively about applicants can be extremely helpful.

How useful tests can be in such circumstances will depend upon the institution's definition of "success," the choice of tests to be used, the quality and scope of local research that precedes and follows test use, the degree to which tests are allowed to supplement or support other criteria of selection, and, of course, the skill with which admissions personnel obtain information from test results for given purposes.

The success criterion

It should be mentioned at the outset that "success" is here defined largely as academic success, for the most common problem faced in admissions is the identification of students who can be graduated under the prevailing academic standard. Beyond that, depending upon the size of its pool of applicants, an institution may further be able to secure such other representation in the make-up of the class as will guarantee leadership in various activities considered important to the college community, a good representation of creative talents or special interests in various fields of endeavor, and the variety of ethnic, religious, economic, and geographic background that ensures the desired degree of cultural representation in the group.

For most institutions, the definition of "success" adopted above is tenable; for others, not completely so. For, at the one extreme, there are those who strive to find not only students who can be graduated with the usual C average, but as many as possible who can be graduated both with grade averages well above minimum and with other attributes signifying a high level of intellectual and social development. At the other extreme, there are institutions with high student mortality rates who, because of local circumstance, may consider themselves fortunate to secure students who have a good chance of remaining just through the early phase of the program; such students may be expected to profit from their briefer educational experience as much in terms of improved attitudes or other personal development as in the kind of academic achievement which is commonly described by grade-point ratios. Between these extremes fall other variations of institutional expectation for entering groups, related either to the educational philosophy of the institution or to local circumstances.

Tests have repeatedly proven their usefulness as predictors of success in the most common academic areas—liberal arts, medicine, dentistry, engineering, law, and nursing. They are being developed rapidly, too, as predictors of academic success in some of the so-called occupational fields, again with the measure of success described either by grade-point ratio in these curricula or by achievement scores in later institution-wide testing. That they do not function at an even higher level of prediction results partly from the failure of colleges to identify clearly for test builders the kind of abilities in their applicants they want differentiated and described and partly from the failure of local methods of evaluation to appraise educational objectives successfully. For these reasons, therefore, tests must be carefully selected in the first place to fit existing circumstances, and their efficiency must be judged in the final analysis only after the local effort to describe student achievement has been perfected. This means then that a prediction test which may be highly successful in one situation does not necessarily apply in another and that each institution needs to weigh local factors carefully in anticipation of setting up an effective admissions testing program.

The selection of the tests

With the perplexing problems of admissions which are currently besetting higher education as a result of the population increase, there is grave danger that an institution may not give sufficient consideration to the characteristics of its student population and its particular program and will be tempted to use tests and standards of selection that have proven successful in institutions which it does not resemble and should not copy. This could only be labeled a mechanical and blind effort to limit numbers that would result in the denial of educational opportunity to the kind of young men and women who in the past had been well qualified to undertake the kind of program the institution offered. It has not yet been shown that the kind of aptitude test that has successfully identified many students who can profit from a liberal arts education of highly abstract emphasis will identify equally well candidates who will be successful in medical technology, agriculture, nursing, education, business administration, and so on. Only an organized effort to identify the intellectual and general characteristics of students successful in these branches of study can contribute to the production of tests needed to select them in the first place. It may be found that existing tests will largely serve the purpose, but until it is so demonstrated, such testing will remain suspect.

An institution that has not utilized tests for admissions might begin by analyzing on an a priori basis the kinds of skills that are required by first-year students. Where stable and fairly valid grading practices are maintained, it has generally been found that first-year performance is a good criterion of success in the remaining college years; therefore, it appears that if admissions criteria can be utilized that describe the skills needed in the first year they will prove useful on a long-term basis also. For this reason, prediction studies can, with some validity and convenience at the outset, be confined to first-year performance.

If the institution is in no position to construct tests to measure the basic skills needed by its freshmen, it will need to examine published tests to see which incorporate the skills and background information considered requisite to the beginning studies of freshmen. Such tests are described in the *Mental Measurements Yearbook*.[1] The kind of tests required will vary greatly from one institution to another. In one, freshmen may take work mainly in general education, for which readiness may best be described by achievement of basic background information in general studies and ability to read and analyze specific materials at a certain level of difficulty; in another institution, freshmen may need to demonstrate readiness for courses in chemistry and mathematics of a specific level. Or perhaps the same institution may have to identify both kinds of groups and therefore need to utilize a greater variety of admissions testing and criteria. The experiences of other colleges of similar purpose who have already used the tests should be solicited. Research data should be sought in the literature or secured from the test publisher. If possible the tests should be given a trial locally with an entering freshman group prior to any final decision on their use. Often they can be incorporated in the orientation-week program of tests usually required of accepted candidates. A few years of trial, or less if the numbers provide a sufficiently large sample, and comparisons with the success criterion (usually grade-point ratios) will reveal their usefulness.

Plans for utilizing data

Statistical methods for analyzing test data for prediction purposes are provided in all textbooks of educational statistics. One of

[1] Oscar K. Buros (ed.), *Fourth Mental Measurements Yearbook*. This book includes more complete descriptions of tests than are found in publishers' catalogues. Included are reviews by one or more critics and references to published research on the tests.

the most clear-cut and detailed descriptions may be found in *Statistics in Education and Psychology* by Garrett.[2] A simplified discussion of the concept of prediction versus chance may be found in a bulletin prepared by a test publisher.[3] The very small institution can often derive great benefit from admissions data by using merely inspection techniques, simple analyses, or even what amounts to a case-study approach. After repeated use, the small institution can also ascertain the reliability of its procedures on a more formal statistical basis. Larger institutions who need to convert data for IBM analysis can obtain special information on that method from a booklet prepared by the American Association of Collegiate Registrars and Admissions Officers.[4]

The agency plan

Few colleges are in a position to administer their own admissions tests; the factor of geography alone is prohibitive. For this reason many college admissions testing programs rely heavily on the special programs of such agencies as the College Entrance Examination Board or those of state-wide testing services or the senior year testing of local high schools. The value of the services of these agencies to an institution can be judged only by the relevance of the tests used to local need, the cost, the security of circulation provided by the agent, and the convenience to prospective applicants. The great majority of colleges now have fairly easy access to some such service. A major disadvantage in some agency and locally administered programs is that students will have had (legitimate) prior experience with the exact tests used, since some tests suitable for admissions purposes may have been used by high school guidance counselors. When admissions tests are handled by the college itself, it should select those that are specifically restricted for college admissions use; participation in agency programs should be restricted to those with adequate security controls.

[2] Henry E. Garrett, *Statistics in Education and Psychology*. See in particular pp. 254 ff. Some may find other texts equally useful.

[3] "Better than Chance," Test Service Bulletin No. 45. Available from the Psychological Corporation upon request.

[4] *Machine Equipment for Efficient Office Operation* (1954). Available from the secretary of the American Association of Collegiate Registrars and Admissions Officers.

THE USE OF TESTS IN SUPPLEMENTING AND CLARIFYING OTHER ADMISSIONS DATA

Regardless of the content of the tests or the sources from which they originate, they must be viewed not as infallible criteria, but as partial criteria to be weighed with other evidence of the applicant's fitness. These other elements may include the applicant's high school grades, the pattern of the courses he has taken, recommendations from his school, the impression he makes in interview, perhaps samples of his writing, his ability to finance his education without undue strain, evidence of his incentive, and results of any other tests that he may already have taken.

Conflicting data

Most of the difficulties which an admissions staff experiences in utilizing the multiple criteria are related fundamentally to the problem of equating these criteria to each other, since they possess as many denominators as there are schools, raters, and test publishers contributing data. Let us consider some of the causes of the discrepancies that will be found.

Primarily, there is an uncontrollable variability in high school grading practices. But these variabilities do not necessarily arise from poor evaluation procedures. What the high school does for the kind of students it has and how it grades them may be quite valid, since not all high schools operate primarily as college-preparatory institutions. Some colleges draw most of their students from a few high schools whose purposes and standards they know well and may therefore be able to use some discrimination in evaluating the grades given. Other colleges that draw their student bodies from a wider radius and so have more high schools to cope with are not in that informed position.[5] Some colleges draw both

[5] For analyzing grade differences among high schools, some colleges have found useful an equating plan developed by the Commission on the Relation of Independent Schools to Higher Education of the National Council of Independent Schools. The material is contained in *Annual Reports of the National Registration Office for Independent Schools,* and shows the kinds of grades obtained at particular colleges by graduates with a given grade average from particular high schools. These *Annual Reports* are issued to member schools of the council. Further information may be obtained from Marjory Etnyre, Secretary, National Registration Office of the National Council of Independent Schools, Room 103, 5801 Ellis Ave., Chicago 37, Ill.

from private college-preparatory institutions of varying quality and from public college-preparatory and nonpreparatory high schools of varying quality. Obviously, many different grading practices will be reflected among the applicants' transcripts.

The problem of controlling the factor of prejudice in personal ratings is also universally recognized. Sometimes a rating can be evaluated in terms of how well known to the admissions personnel the individual rater may be. The rating of an experienced admissions counselor can be wrong, too, if, for example, he has had to formulate an opinion when the applicant was accompanied to the interview by a domineering parent.

The contribution to the total picture of all previously obtained test data of the student's high school career can lend further support if the situation is clear-cut. But such test data require much skill in interpretation, since in working with the multiple kinds of test data found on transcripts, the interpreter must have a thorough appreciation for the differences in normative groups and be able to use quite a collection of manuals and norms booklets. Unless his training has been specialized, the usual admissions director flounders at this point.

It is much simpler to have one set of appropriate tests given to all applicants at an identical point in their development and to use these as the common denominator for evaluating some of the complicating credentials of ratings, grading standards, and multiple test reports.

Sorting and follow-up

If experience has been had in using known tests, rational cutting points, and supplementary data supplied by the high school, it has been found that as high as 50 to 70 percent of applicants can be identified fairly easily as suitable or completely unsuitable prospective students, and so promptly encouraged or discouraged. Thereafter, delay in acceptance is likely to be related to the assembly of the applicant's complete dossier, to "contract" agreements with other colleges on filing dates, or to the student's own indecision about his choice than to any difficulty of decision about his acceptability. After this first screening, the remaining decisions are quite difficult and may revolve about one of several questions.

For example, there may be an applicant from a high school unknown to the admissions office whose admissions test reports, previous test data supplied by the school, or the principal's rating conflict with the high school grade report; if the admissions test scores seem poor in the face of other data, retesting through a special arrangement with a high school officer may clear up the discrepancy. In retesting, it may be desirable to try the student on nonspeeded tests, if speed of work is not an important criterion of success at the particular college, or to arrange for a selection of tests more suitable to the individual situation than those represented in the regular admissions battery.

Another difficulty arises when there is a surplus of seemingly equally well-qualified applicants, a situation encountered usually in choosing among applicants for scholarships. Needless to say, the more definitive the test data that can be secured, the easier the selection of final candidates. For this reason many institutions require that scholarship applicants take tests that are additional to the regularly required battery.

There are usually a few cases where a personal rating of one individual rater raises doubt about a candidate whose qualifications may otherwise seem excellent. A good high school record supported by acceptable admissions test data has undoubtedly saved more than one prospective candidate from the ire of a rater, who may for unjust reasons have attacked the candidate's fitness. Rechecks of such ratings through special correspondence are in order.

Special cases in applicant evaluation

Finally, supplementary tests can be of help in handling those special applicants whose background may be completely alien to that covered by the admissions tests used, yet whose preparation to undertake advanced studies may be entirely adequate. After all, tests designed for general admissions uses must be tailored to fit the common preparation that most students do receive and they are standardized for such groups; therefore, they should not be expected to serve as well for the qualified applicant who has received his education in what might be termed an unorthodox fashion.

For example, there may be precocious non-high-school graduates who can demonstrate that they are well enough equipped to undertake the program; similarly, there may be a few applicants, part of whose preparatory work was in business subjects, who can demonstrate achievement of the basic skills and interests that compensate for the few units they lack; there are adults who may have an advantage in preparation and others with a discrepancy resulting from delays in their formal education; and there are international students who need to determine their readiness for an American education and the level at which they should enter.

Another group of special applicants that can be better handled with recourse to tests are the transfer cases. Some institutions have but few of these, but there are many others, particularly those fed by neighboring junior colleges, who accept a great many transfer students, and sometimes have even more transfer students in their upper classes than they have students who entered as freshmen. Such institutions can, through the use of some such battery as the National College Sophomore Testing Program, the Graduate Record Area Examinations, or other tests they consider to be more appropriate to their own basic curriculum requirements, make a reliable selection among the applicants.

Occasionally an institution may wish to consider a doubtful transfer applicant, say, one who has not done well elsewhere in terms of grade average but who, for reasons that need not be developed here, deserves a second chance. Take, for example, the transfer student who brings an F or an Incomplete in two courses, which he received for not submitting, because of an accident, the final course term papers. While, at most institutions, he probably could not be allowed credit for these courses, he might through examination demonstrate his competence in the basic skills and content encompassed and so be allowed to utilize them to fulfill college prerequisite requirements.

These several descriptions of solutions to problem cases have been developed to demonstrate the general usefulness of tests in certain dilemmas that arise in unusual instances. In all these cases, it might be pointed out, not only has the institution gained, but the applicant also has usually improved his ability to accept whatever decision is made and undertakes with greater confidence what is for him a new experience in adjustment.

THE ADMINISTRATION OF THE ADMISSIONS TESTING PROGRAM

A college that decides to incorporate tests in its admissions program must design administrative procedures to support their best functioning. If admissions tests are required, that fact should be mentioned in the college catalogue; potential applicants should be informed as early and as clearly as is possible about the nature of the tests, when and where they may be taken, what they will cost, and what bearing they will have on the final decision to be made.

Provisions must be made for the integration of the admissions test data with the other data about the applicant. Usually, all are assembled simply in one folder along with all correspondence with the student, his high school, and his parents. If resources permit, it is advisable that one qualified person summarize all test data of an applicant on one report sheet, so that they will not be scattered throughout the folder and so that they receive closer consideration than time permits in the usual admissions committee meeting. Most of the admissions test data will subsequently be useful in the general guidance of accepted candidates; thus, provisions should be made for transferring the roster of test results to appropriate college offices and faculty advisers for permanent retention.

If the college receives and attempts to utilize test data from several or more sources—say, the various College Entrance Examination Board programs, the Independent High School Testing Program of the Educational Records Bureau, the Differential Aptitude Tests data supplied by a high school, and, perhaps, the data obtained in one of the several state-wide programs—it is advisable to assemble in advance whatever information is needed to interpret the normative data supplied for each test and if possible to attempt in advance some rough equating of such data to data that may already exist for students currently enrolled in the institution. Each institution can in time build up its own norms so that it need not be dependent on the shifting bases of national norms or the special bases of norms for particular kinds of students.

In advance of final decisions, the admissions personnel can rank students roughly into several or more categories of acceptability in line with principles previously established by the governing group.

Tests must *not* be viewed as the ready-made, flawless answer to admissions puzzles; they supply substantial clues in each situation, but their application has limitations not always readily apparent to the uninitiated. Tests are more likely to fail because of misuse by those who hoped for a short cut in analysis than because of shortcomings not made explicit in the data provided by the publisher. Therefore, if the admissions staff does not include a qualified test specialist, there should be easy access to the institution's test officer, or, if there is none, to a qualified consultant who can lend occasional help.

Once effective procedures for handling admissions test data are developed, the procedures should not be allowed to become mechanical or routine. The three important elements of the process —the program of the institution, the caliber of the applicant group in general, and the success criterion of the institution—can and probably will change with time. There is thus good reason to reconsider the elements periodically and every reason to subject all admissions practices, including the tests and test procedures utilized, to reappraisal.

FURTHER READING

There are other discussions on the subject of admissions testing that the interested reader will want to examine. For several years the College Entrance Examination Board has published the papers delivered at its annual colloquia on college admissions problems.[6] The papers present a multitude of considerations and procedures of general interest to admissions personnel and are well worth scanning for those of definite local application. A discussion by Chauncey and Frederiksen in *Educational Measurement*[7] elabo-

---

[6] *College Admissions 1, 2, 3,* and *4.* College Entrance Examination Board, Box 592, Princeton, N.J.

[7] Henry Chauncey and Norman Frederiksen, "The Function of Measurement in Educational Placement," in E. F. Lindquist (ed.), *Educational Measurement,* pp. 85 ff.

rates many of the points that have had but brief mention here; in particular, their discussion of the reliability of high school rank and their discussion of admissions to special college programs within the university are illuminating. A simple beginning to the statistics of prediction has been given by Cronbach.[8] The works mentioned contain bibliographies. Persons responsible for the formulation and execution of admissions policies can keep informed on relevant issues, reported in the *College Board Review*.[9]

[8] Lee J. Cronbach, "Treatment of Data in Prediction Studies" and "Principles of Prediction," *Essentials of Psychological Testing*, pp. 247 ff.

[9] *College Board Review*. Published three times a year by the College Entrance Examination Board; subscription offices, P.O. Box 592, Princeton, N.J.

3. The Use of Tests in Course Placement or Accreditation

As useful as the admissions and guidance programs of a college may be in helping generally to promote optimum learning and to reduce student failure, the range of abilities among students in a particular class or program of study may still be wide. It is very difficult to bridge the gaps in learning that occur with students whose abilities, preparation for a course, and interests vary greatly. Sometimes greater individualization of instruction is achieved by establishing numerous small sections; perhaps this is the ideal solution, but it is one that is not practicable for most colleges. Therefore, many institutions have instead adopted a policy of placing students in course sections representing different degrees of attainment so that instruction may proceed at the level appropriate to the capacity or readiness of the group.

STEPS IN THE PLACEMENT PROCEDURE

In almost all colleges there are certain courses which practically all, if not all, freshmen and sophomores are required to take because their content and purposes are considered essential. In some, the purpose is to provide important and basic general background which students, if left to their own initiative of electing courses, might not obtain; in others, the major purpose is to develop skills and acquire knowledge needed for subsequent courses. Regardless of the reason, the result is that at most institutions more students are enrolled in certain courses of the first two years than can readily be accommodated in single instructional units. Thus, there is a need to establish some basis for sectioning students into smaller units.

If it is decided that placement in a course is to be made on the basis of homogeneity, then an analysis of the abilities and background required for success in the course is necessary. What general skills and how much specific knowledge are necessary to enable the student to make best progress from his current level? Theoretically, where selective admissions criteria are employed and if the criteria have been good, any student should be able to complete any required course. But the issue in point is to have him do so with maximum opportunity for progress and without interference to or from fellow students. It is not always necessary that each class unit be handled in exactly the same way, even though the general course objective may be identical for all; both content and method can be varied depending upon the readiness of students. A course in first-year chemistry for premedical students may be quite different from a course in beginning chemistry for the student of agronomy; a course in the development of social institutions can be taught largely by a discussion method to students of certain reading sophistication and some demonstrated knowledge of the subject, with greater enrichment for them, but this may not be the best approach for students of lesser background, alertness, and interest in the field.

A first step in the placement procedure, then, is to determine what talents a student should possess, or just what he should be able to do, to derive optimum benefit from the course as it will be arranged. Arrangement, of course, is contingent upon local resources for making optimum provisions. Once the expected preparation or abilities have been defined, attention can be directed to selecting or constructing tests suitable for establishing their attainment. Frequently, and more often than is commonly assumed, some of the tests used in an entrance program may be further used successfully for purposes of placement and acceleration. Sometimes, other data, such as high school grades in related subjects, can supplement test data.

The identification of criteria for placement is first established on an a priori basis with time eventually dictating their usefulness. They may prove ineffective because of poor initial choice, poor instruction, or poor methods of evaluating course success; all three factors then must be considered in reappraising the placement criteria.

Fortunately, there are a number of tests available that are quite suitable for placement purposes at the college freshman level;

these identify general aptitudes, skills, and background achievement. The number of units of high school study and the quality of achievement as indicated by the high school grade (where the standard of the high school grade is known) also contribute to a more accurate understanding of the individual student's readiness. Locally constructed examinations, built up from past examination materials of the course will add another dimension to the evaluative data. In fact, it is probably quite safe to assert that as far as placement in course is concerned, there are much more data available for use than many an institution is able to utilize.

WAIVING REQUIRED COURSES

Frequently it may be desirable to waive required courses if students have already mastered the skills and learning which the courses are intended to develop. When this is done, some basis other than course grades is needed to place the exempted students in an intermediate or advanced course. In some instances, the final examination for Course A may serve as a basis for waiving that prerequisite. In many cases, however, it will be inappropriate, especially if the prerequisite is being waived without credit. Then, one simply wants to know if a given student has adequately mastered the elements that are essential to a subsequent course. Certain aspects of Course A may be more important for success in Course B than other aspects of Course A. If this is the case, an examination for granting credit in Course A would cover more material than is necessary for determining placement in the subsequent course. Consequently, a student might not do well on the test for granting credit, primarily because of failure on the materials not important for placement purposes, and yet be quite capable of doing satisfactory work in the subsequent course. An examination geared to the elements considered essential for success in the second course would then be more appropriate.

Sometimes even when one of the purposes of a prerequisite course is to develop abilities required in subsequent courses, an able student may be able to compensate rather quickly for his lack of formal background. On the basis of his superior ability, he may be able to keep up quite well with the average student who has had the required special training in the prerequisite course. Here aptitude alone may be a sufficient basis for waiving a prerequisite. However, entrance into the subsequent course should be based on aptitude alone only if there is adequate evidence that students with a high level of general aptitude can actually perform successfully in the course without previously having acquired the prerequisite knowledge or skills.

PLACEMENT IN SPECIFIC COURSES

Placement in freshman English

Since freshman English is the most generally required subject in college, placement activity in this area is probably greater than in any other college course.

A college is seldom able to establish more than three freshman English groups: superior, average, and below average. The criteria ordinarily employed are: (1) senior English grades from high schools whose grading standards are known, since they give at little cost a relatively dependable picture of the student's most recent performance; (2) a measure of scholastic aptitude, probably available from entrance test data; this may be a total score, or, if the test has a verbal and a quantitative section, only the verbal score, since it indicates the extent to which the student understands and is able to deal with verbal relationships; and (3) scores from an English test administered for admission or as part of the freshman guidance test program. When such scores are not available from some other institutional testing program, the department may administer a local or published test on the fundamentals of English, or one aimed more directly at writing ability, depending upon the objectives of the course and what is expected of the beginning student.

Placement in foreign languages

Foreign languages also rank high, insofar as placement or the waiving of courses is concerned, because here success in subsequent courses also depends directly upon skills built in earlier courses. If students come from a variety of secondary schools with varying quality of foreign language instruction, some standard basis for assessing the level at which they should continue study is most desirable.

Examinations of proficiency in vocabulary, grammar, and reading and aural comprehension will readily supply the information needed for assigning students to a beginning course or to a course aimed at developing basic skills at a somewhat higher level, or to a conversation course, or to one of the several literature courses. Cutting points for determining these various assignments are best fixed by first using the tests in the courses with regularly enrolled students as their final examination and determining the correlation between their proficiency and the test results.

Placement in other courses

The problem of placement in *mathematics* resembles that in foreign languages since most colleges offer a uniform sequence of courses with progress in subsequent courses dependent upon success in preceding ones. Consequently, it is relatively easy to select or to develop a test which covers the material appropriate for one or more of these courses.

In the *natural sciences* the problem is more complex. In many institutions, there is a variety of science offerings, with one course for the student with no background, another for the nonmajor who has had a high school course, still another for the pre-engineer, and a fourth for the potential major. Furthermore, for certain of these, specific mathematical skills may be required. In more advanced chemistry courses, there may be prerequisites from other fields of science. In a situation as complex as this, it is most important to analyze carefully the intended value of the prerequisites and the extent to which the subsequent course really requires the knowledge and skills developed in the prerequisite course. Usually, the requirement of a prerequisite high school course can be waived for students with high scientific aptitude, especially, if, as is often true, the college course really starts all over again and proceeds at a much faster pace for those who have had previous work. In many science courses, quantitative aptitude is likely to be important, but seldom to the exclusion of verbal aptitude. Specific tests of scientific aptitude are available or can be constructed. A combination of these, selected empirically and utilized along with careful and thorough content analysis, solves many placement problems. In the more advanced science courses, the work is much more likely to begin at a specific level, since there is certainty that all students will have reached this point. Here tests of achievement are likely to be much more effective for placement or screening than are tests of aptitude.

Placement in the *social sciences* and the *humanities* is similar in some respects but different from that discussed so far. These disciplines are much less likely to have a standard sequence of courses, each a prerequisite for the one following. Individual courses are much more likely to be self-contained. Course prerequisites more often serve to ensure general familiarity with the vocabulary, tools, and concepts of the subject. If this is the case, an aptitude test and a general test covering vocabulary, tools, and concepts may be appropriate for determining admission to advanced courses.

MEETING DEGREE AND HONORS REQUIREMENTS THROUGH EXAMINATIONS

At times it may be appropriate to grant a student credit in a course without his taking it if he demonstrates a particular level of competency. Or it may be desirable to know that each student has achieved a certain minimum level of general education before he is admitted to the upper division of the college, or to have him demonstrate a high level of achievement before granting him honors. Each of these situations poses its own problems, different from those already discussed, though there are some similarities in procedure if tests are used as a major criterion. Let us, then, review them in at least a general way.

The granting of course credit on the basis of examination alone has not been widely practiced, although it may develop momentum. This lag has been partly due to a definite rejection of the idea by college faculties and partly to the fact that so few students have sought the opportunity. However, there is a growing emphasis in some high schools on providing enriched or college-level courses for superior students,[1] who may in turn wish to accelerate their

[1] See College Entrance Examination Board, *Advanced Placement Program* and Charles R. Keller, "Piercing the Sheepskin Curtain," in *College Board Review*, Fall 1956, p. 1.

The report of the Ford Foundation, *They Went to College Early*, Evaluation Report No. 2, on the Program for Early Admission to College will also be of

college work and will apply for admission to those colleges that offer that opportunity. Even though the proportion of students in this category remains relatively low, colleges hoping to provide diversified programs for expanding student enrollments may explore the feasibility of granting credit on the basis of adequate performance on a test designed for the purpose.

The superior entering student is not the only kind of student who may seek credit by examination. There are other situations in which either the student, the college, or both may consider the possibility of an accreditation by means of examination. Sometimes, students, because of illness or financial reverses, find it necessary to leave college before the completion of a semester or a year of course work; when they are able to return, they may wish to advance with the students in their class or at least to have an opportunity to make up some of the credits they have lost in the areas in which they feel most confident. Transfer students who believe that they have already covered certain prerequisites in another sequence of courses may wish to receive credit toward their degree without taking (and possibly repeating) the sequence required in the new college. Or the college itself, uncertain of how to appraise the past work of transfer students in relation to particular required courses, may need to have students demonstrate the extent to which they have mastered major outcomes before granting credit.

Whatever the reasons for setting up a program of credit by examination, the major problem facing the college will be that of ascertaining whether given students have achieved a level of competency equivalent to that achieved by those who have taken the course or courses in question. This problem is quite similar to that of waiving prerequisites without credit. The major difference lies in the extent to which the outcomes of the course must be measured. In waiving a required course, it may be necessary to be concerned only with evaluating skills and learning that are essential to success in subsequent courses. In granting credit, these elements, together with other major achievements the course is intended to develop, must be measured. Assurance is needed that the students who receive credit by examination are as competent as those who

interest to those who are considering the early admission of superior candidates. Available from the Fund for the Advancement of Education, 477 Madison Ave., New York 21, N.Y.

have taken the course. Thus, an examination designed for waiving the course will not necessarily satisfy the requirements for granting credit; a separate and somewhat more comprehensive examination is needed. Also, some outcomes may be demonstrated only when certain projects, such as written reports, are completed. This could be made a requirement additional to examination performance.

As in placement programs, the first step should be a thorough analysis of the content of the course in question. When the analysis has been systematically made, it is then possible to review existing tests to determine the extent to which they correspond to the goals of the course. A natural temptation will be to use an existing course final examination as a basis for awarding credit. If the final examination is already the sole basis for awarding grade and credit in the course, it would be difficult to make a case against using it without at the same time requiring some revision in the present course.

However, the final examination is not usually the sole basis for awarding credit. There may be other examinations during the course, term papers, projects, or other assignments, and classroom discussions, all of which may serve as partial bases for evaluating the student's performance. If evaluation based on these is believed to be essential in determining whether or not the objectives of the course have been attained, then a way must be found to incorporate into the examination for credit some measure of their accomplishment. It may well be, in some cases, that an examination cannot stand in place of the course itself because too much of the course depends upon participation in the group growth and development and the general maturation that comes with systematic exposure to a body of ideas and knowledge. It also may be believed that there are intangibles that are acquired by exposure during the course and that cannot be measured by an examination.

This last answer should not be accepted too readily, however; the intangibles may not be measurable because they are not there to begin with. Most instructors believe that their own courses actually accomplish much more than meets the eye. If the assertion is made that there are things that cannot be measured, then it is obviously impossible to prove or to disprove successfully the assertion that they are being acquired. The question, then, should not be whether every possible benefit from the course is subject to testing but whether an examination can be obtained or constructed that evaluates the broad, important outcomes expected from the course. Usually this can be done; but frequently it will be different from the regular final examination given in the course. It may be that a published test or a test prepared by another college offering a similar course will be appropriate. Just as often, it may be necessary to construct a special test which will reflect the broad instructional outcomes of the course.

A problem almost as crucial as the determination of the nature of the examination is the determination of the score level required for the granting of credit. A range of scores will be obtained in practice, and some cutting point must be determined so that scores above this level will establish credit and scores below will not. As mentioned earlier, for many courses there will be relatively few students requesting the opportunity to gain credit by examination. This means that the data obtained from actual use of the test will remain quite meager for some time after its introduction—a major advantage of using an already developed test on which some norms are available. The latter might be either a published test with so-called national norms, or a test prepared for similar courses in another college or university. In either case, there is likely to be some indication of how a known group of students has performed on it.

One could, of course, on a subjective basis alone, specify the level of achievement a student must reach to receive credit for the course. Although this approach has merit, in practice it has certain shortcomings. The desired level of accomplishment might be set at a level higher than that actually achieved by even the best students who take the course. It is, therefore, wise to study the test results to see whether students taking the course do perform at the specified level of competency.

If there are a number of different expected outcomes for the course, and if they are not necessarily closely related, it is reasonable to require the student to achieve a passing score in each. This will ensure that he has covered the broad objectives of the course and not passed simply on the basis of high proficiency in one narrow aspect. If the decision is made to use multiple cutting scores in this fashion, one should be sure that the individual subtests on which the separate scores are based are sufficiently dependable to use as a basis for withholding or granting credit.

COMPREHENSIVE EXAMINATIONS IN PLACEMENT

In some institutions fulfillment of the objectives of basic courses at minimum levels only may be deemed an insufficient attainment to warrant the student's entering upon advanced study in the area or entering upon a major study in that area, and examinations can be used in reaching the decision. The point must be made, however, that it is not the suggestion here that examinations alone be used without recourse to other criteria such as teacher recommendations.

If a college contemplates such a move, it will do well to try its examinations experimentally, keeping in view that the screening points must be set realistically to be consonant with the institution's objectives. Again, examinations may be selected from published examinations or be constructed to suit local needs; also, in either case, a decision should be made as to whether the content of the tests shall be general or specific in nature.

The institution that decides to use examinations on a "general" basis may administer, for example, some such general battery as the National College Sophomore Tests, the Graduate Record Area Examination, or the Sequential Tests of Educational Progress. Adopting a basis that, in the experience of the institution, has some validity, it may be found that few, if any, students below a certain score on any one of these examinations or its separate parts are good risks as advanced students, and they should, therefore, not be encouraged to continue. Or an alternative may be permitted: they may be conditioned, that is, allowed to continue with the understanding that they will be expected to do additional work to remedy the deficiency disclosed. For example, if a student passes in all subjects except mathematics and if the college considers proficiency in mathematics to be essential to the degree it wishes to underwrite, then the student may be required to satisfy the examination in mathematics sometime prior to graduation. In any event, the faculty must first determine its own standards of performance, and it follows that these should be realistic for the student group served by the institution.

The foregoing is an example of a general requirement rather than one worked out specifically for a particular department. The latter can be illustrated by a program designed for selecting students for a secondary teacher education training program. Here, while several additional criteria of ability and personality would undoubtedly also be considered, tests in English, speech, fundamentals of education, and general culture could be used and it might be agreed, in line with the general thinking of the college in the matter, that prospective teachers should be expected to be prepared at somewhat higher levels than others, and the standard set, therefore, at a higher level. In the case of an elementary education student, it might be decided to include an examination in mathematics in the criteria for selection.

Similarly, tests can be utilized at the time of graduation to screen applicants who should not be graduated because they fail to meet important objectives at an achievement level deemed appropriate for a graduate of the institution. Any of the batteries of examinations listed above might be used for this purpose; in addition, it is probable that an examination in the major subject should be added.

Since all the considerations of good test selection or construction that have been presented in connection with other phases of the discussion in the present work are applicable in any of these situations, they will not be reviewed. It should suffice to summarize the general approach as being one that requires (1) the identification of the skills, abilities, attitudes, or other attributes considered relevant, (2) the selection or construction of the tests and other criteria that will help describe their attainment at whatever level is established as locally appropriate, and (3) the fixing of the critical passing scores on empirical bases.

4. The Use of Tests in Instruction

A GREAT DEAL OF THE INFORMATION THAT IS COLLECTED IN THE process of testing for admissions and placement purposes also finds uses in instruction. Available even prior to instruction, general information about a particular set of students describing their scholastic aptitude, their previous achievement in the field, their reading level, their English skills, and so on can assist an instructor in gauging the general level at which he can teach a class and identifiy those who are deficient or advanced. Even though his circumstances may not be such that he can provide ideally for each group, he at least possesses a more informed understanding of them. The economics instructor should be alerted to the fact that most of those enrolled in his course are superior students excused from a required beginning course and, at the other extreme, an English instructor with a group whose achievement in English is predominantly low should be aware of his problem from the outset. The extent to which members of an instructional staff can receive initial cueing will be determined, of course, by the quality and extent of local testing programs and by the procedures for channeling data to them.

PURPOSES OF TESTS IN INSTRUCTION

Tests serve in instruction to clarify goals, to determine the initial status of students, to appraise student growth throughout the course, to appraise instructional materials and methods, and to stimulate learning. Each of these purposes will be treated here in some detail.

To clarify the goals of instruction

Instructors teach to increase their students' appreciation of literature, or their understanding of physical laws, or their ability to think straight, or to help them attain equally worthy goals. Ideally, the content and organization of instruction should, in all logic, be derived from its ultimate goals, and evidence should be obtained to demonstrate that they do operate to achieve them. But too frequently this relationship is ignored, and the instructor is content with an abstract and often vague statement of ultimate goals and selects content and method on a basis of tradition or opinion only.

If there were no necessity to appraise student progress, goals could easily remain at an abstract level. Fortunately, the examination of student attainment of basic instructional goals is a fairly universal requirement in higher education, and in the process, goals of instruction must be translated into the more specific behaviors that students demonstrate by doing, thinking, or reacting in some manner.

Thus, for example, in a course where one of the goals of instruction is the development of critical thinking, students are expected to learn to examine certain material and to criticize it from certain points of view. Therefore, in a class exercise their attention may be directed to the material and an effort made to elicit their critical response. One student volunteers a comment; another adds a thought, and the instructor's skillful questioning induces other students to evaluate the adequacy of the material; finally, a satisfactory conclusion is drawn, the instructor summarizes what has been said and makes an additional, more penetrating analysis. Although the instructor may feel generally pleased with the way in which the students have analyzed the problem, even though all students did not participate, how can he be sure that the class as a whole actually did benefit by the example he used? Obviously, by testing with similar sets of material and seeking critical reactions, he will be in a position to review student responses and can then determine whether they actually mastered the objective. If they did not, an analysis of their responses may indicate some of the causes of failure, and the goal, the materials, or the method modified for a fresh trial.

This example illustrates the ideal sequence of stating and examining a goal—namely, defining what it is, selecting materials and exercises, identifying the student behavior which demonstrate its attainment, and ending with appropriate evaluation. But in practice it is rarely possible to proceed so smoothly. Rather, a goal is stated and then, in selecting appropriate teaching material, it may be found that the goal needs further clarification. Or, in preparing the evaluation, it may be recognized that certain of the assignments are unsuited to the development of some of the specific skills. Or, in reviewing student responses to the problem presented by the test question, it may be found that the goal is unrealistic in terms of what students are able to accomplish. Thus, a constant interaction will occur among the various processes which eventually leads to modifications, and a clearer statement of the aims, content, and methods of the course should emerge. In this frame the purposes of achievement testing are much more fundamental in instruction than is indicated in the more commonly stated purpose of grading students.[1]

To determine initial status

While college courses of instruction universally assume the existence of certain initial background on the part of students, it is helpful to know that all students really possess this background.

Pretests, either locally constructed or of the standardized variety, can be of great use in ascertaining this. In addition to information about the class level and about individuals in the class that can be gleaned from any general test programs of the college, the instructor may use special tests to obtain information on the more specific knowledge, skills, and abilities of individual students in relation to his subject, so that he may determine his most suitable course of action.

There are several possible alternatives which might follow upon measurement of initial status. One is that students with insufficient background will be excluded from the course, for it is not always possible to bridge their deficiencies; the physics instructor cannot stop to teach algebra to students who have not mastered the minimum essentials nor can the literature instructor wait for the mastery of reading skill. But even if obviously incompetent students are eliminated, considerable differences among the remaining students may still exist. The particular starting point and the particular sequence of a course should be, so far as possible,

---

[1] For a further development of this process, see Ralph W. Tyler, "Measurement in Improving Instruction," in E. F. Lindquist (ed.), *Educational Measurement*, pp. 49 ff.

adapted to their status. It is well then for the literature instructor to know how much emphasis he will need to give to classical allusions and for the Spanish instructor to know what Spanish vocabulary has been mastered by his beginning second-year class. Some students will be found to be minimally prepared; others may already have mastered minimum goals. If the latter are to be profitably engaged, either they must be given opportunity to pursue additional work within the framework of the course or they must be placed in more advanced courses.

To measure terminal status and growth

How much knowledge students have acquired during the course and to what extent they have achieved course goals are questions which are directly or implicitly raised when final grades are being determined. Test data frequently are not the sole determiners of course grades, but normally they make a relatively major contribution. How test grades will be combined with other evidences of achievement such as term papers and special projects will vary with the policies and practices of the department or institution. Thus, for a freshman English composition course, greater weight may be given to a major primary source paper and to weekly compositions than to the final examination on the assumption that these projects offer a more extensive measure of student writing than can the limited examination; in other courses, the final examination may carry equal or greater weight than other work.

Where it is of interest to determine how much students have really learned in a particular course, as distinct from what they already knew, a measure of status at the end of the course should be related to a measure of beginning status. Thus, a test very similar to the final examination should be administered as a pretest to establish some base line for the measurement of growth.

Also, there are some rather basic educational advantages in obtaining measures of progress on individual students, especially for students who start rather low on the achievement ladder and who, at the end of the course, still appear relatively low when compared with other students. Some of these students may actually have learned a great deal more than is revealed by their final grades, which normally reflect only their rank on some "absolute" scale or in comparison with other students. Growth measures may help to show these students that they actually have benefited from the course and will thus encourage them. They also provide data which aids the instructor in planning appropriate educational experiences in his course.

Although there are advantages in charting student progress, there are certain technical problems which complicate the interpretation of scores. It often happens that students with the lowest scores in an initial test show relatively greater gains than students whose initial scores, while low, were not quite so low and that students who originally earned very high scores earn somewhat lower scores at a second testing, even after instruction. At first glance, it may seem that the poorest students progressed most, while those who were best performers at the outset made no progress, in fact, regressed from original achievement. Logic would question this, and it should, for, indeed, this is not the interpretation that is justified, regardless of appearances. What is often being demonstrated by such score patterns is simply a phenomenon known as "regression toward the mean," which stems largely from inaccuracy of measurement. Tests never provide more than a sampling of all the tasks that an individual could be asked to perform. He might perform somewhat differently on a second, though quite similar, set of tasks and earn a quite different score. He might undertake the same or a similar test with a quite different attitude or motive, or any number of other factors—all beyond our control —might operate to affect the final result. At best, then, a test score is only an estimate of a person's true achievement.

For any individual, scores from separate testings may vary in either direction. When these initial scores are quite different from the score which represents the average performance of a group, there is greater likelihood that a second score will move in the direction of this average rather than away from it; second scores are often somewhat higher than original very low scores and somewhat lower than original very high scores, due to chance variations. This statistical phenomenon will be found discussed in any textbook on statistics.[2]

---

[2] See also "How Accurate Is a Test Score?" *Test Service Bulletin*, No. 50, June 1956. Available from the Psychological Corporation, 522 Fifth Ave., New York, N.Y.

Suffice it to say that such measures can be used as a rough guide to development, provided score differences are large enough to warrant the assumption that they are due to more than chance alone and provided the tests or evaluation devices are inclusive and comprehensive enough to cover what has been taught and experienced in the course. If the course goals have been clearly defined in terms of student behavior, and if the evaluation tasks have been carefully selected to reflect the content and emphases of the course, rather than the general objectives which could be achieved without the course, the score differences should provide the basis for judgment about the progress of students even though precision of measurement is not as refined as might be desired.

To evaluate teaching materials and procedures

It frequently happens that the teacher whose course is well planned and organized assumes that his materials and procedures are satisfactory and that any lack of progress on the part of students results from student ineptitude. But the conscientious instructor must also wonder if his instruction is at fault. With the use of suitable tests or assignments he can determine whether certain approaches have induced good learning experiences. If learning seems inadequate, he will seek a new way to accomplish his goals of instruction. Thus the creative instructor will constantly set up and check hypotheses of the effectiveness of his instruction and modify his procedures in the light of what he finds; in this process, tests can be his chief source of evidence.

To stimulate and guide learning

Tests are useful in stimulating the learning of students. The student's concept of course goals is fixed largely by the examinations used, and the kind of examination used influences the way in which students will study. While the teaching aim for a course may be to develop critical thinking ability, if the course tests require the recall of somebody else's conclusions based on their critical thinking or if it requires primarily the recall of the information prerequisite to critical thinking about a topic, students will, in their future study, focus on learning the information they will need for such answers. If, on the other hand, test questions are framed so that the student is required to organize and relate information in a manner requiring his own independent critical thinking, there is much greater likelihood that he will, in his study, practice the critical analysis of materials.

If tests are to serve as guides to study, it is necessary that they be used periodically throughout the course. Some instructors have found it helpful to provide practice test questions for students, particularly if the form of test varies much from the forms the students are acquainted with. Usually some discussion takes place in advance of the examination, designed to help the student in his preparation. The variation of examination form to prevent over-emphasis on one narrow type of preparation is sometimes effective in forcing students to consider material from different angles.

When students are given an opportunity to test their learning by responding to test questions or other evaluative devices, when they learn whether or not their responses are correct, and when they have an opportunity to correct misinformation, there is greater advance in learning than when they lack these opportunities. There is much to be said for the discussion and analysis of the examination answers in a later class meeting, and, as a by-product, the instructor also has an opportunity to learn why students answered questions in a particular way. This often gives him insight into the good points or shortcomings of some of his methods or highlights some of the weaknesses of the test questions and leads to the improvement of learning exercises and test questions in the future.

Returning tests and discussing test questions in class poses a problem for the instructor who maintains a test file for future use, for copies of the used questions may fall into the hands of future students and threaten test security. One way to circumvent this difficulty is to maintain two files of alternate test questions designed to measure the same skills and abilities. The second file would serve the class discussion purpose. Another way is to discuss the test in general in class without the actual return of papers; after all, the student will recall his errors and from the point of view that any test is a mere sample of a larger body of content, providing answers for this fragment assumes much less importance. A third method is to make available so comprehensive a file of questions that the entire course is encompassed.

THE ADVANTAGES AND DISADVANTAGES
OF STANDARDIZED TESTS

It is quite obvious that the content of published tests may not be suited to measuring attainment of all the objectives that a particular instructor envisages for his class. Yet, such tests may possess certain valuable characteristics which teacher-made tests do not have.

A well-constructed standardized test has the advantage of having been planned by a representative group of subject-matter specialists. Because it is designed for use at different institutions, it is likely to emphasize important goals of achievement that are independent of particular textbooks and scholastic prejudices. It serves as an independent check on student progress and helps identify any important aspects of study that are being overlooked. A standardized test, because of the care with which it has been constructed, usually possesses technical characteristics that assure a more dependable measurement. There is an added advantage in the opportunity afforded through its norms to compare the class with students trained elsewhere. Further, because it has had the advantage of tryout, it is freer of ambiguous questions and of questions that fail to discriminate between good and poor students.

On the other hand, the published test cannot reflect the unique emphases of particular courses. Because it is designed for use with large numbers, it is usually of a nature which permits measurement of general rather than highly specific goals. But the greatest disadvantage of all is the paucity of such tests designed for use in specific college courses. Except for tests in so-called freshman English, in mathematics, in chemistry, and in foreign languages, the representation is most limited. There continues to be a great need for the development of tests in such universally appearing subjects in college curricula as principles of economics, principles of sociology, American literature, English, United States history, logic, history of philosophy, educational psychology, general psychology, Shakespeare, Chaucer, and many others. It is a time-consuming task for the instructor to prepare a sound classroom test; if a basic test were available, he could devote his energies to the preparation of the supplemental tests needed for special aspects of his course.

THE DEVELOPMENT OF LOCAL EXAMINATIONS

Since it is most unlikely that he will find entirely suitable tests elsewhere, the instructor must eventually draft his own quizzes, tests, and examinations. If his materials and assignments have been selected in relation to well thought-out goals, including a precise statement of changes expected in student behavior, much of the basic material for his task is already available. The problem then becomes one of organizing this material in such a manner that good questions will be produced. A good test plan will indicate in detail what it is that the test will measure and will try to formulate answers to such questions as: What are the objectives being sought? How does the student show that he has achieved these instructional goals? Which of these behaviors can be measured by the indirect method that the written test situation imposes? To what extent can the test exercises be made to approximate the actual behavior? Is it feasible to substitute test demonstrations for paper-and-pencil tests? (This is seldom practicable, except on an occasional basis to determine the extent to which the written test is a proper or improper substitute for the true demonstration of achievement.) Should the test measure the extent to which a limited number of objectives or a certain unit of the course has been mastered, or will it attempt to cover more of the course? Will the test focus primarily on ability to reproduce content which has been covered specifically, or will it attempt to measure the ability of the student to apply what has been taught to new materials?

It is rarely possible to build a test without altering its original plan from time to time. For example, in identifying concrete situations to demonstrate the attainment of a particular goal, the plan may begin to show insufficient detail or a question will emerge in writing which is good and obviously suitable, but it may be found that no category exists for classifying it. It may then be realized that a quite valid goal or category has been overlooked in the listing, and it will consequently be added. Thus, continual inter-action of the various steps in the process leads to a general clarifica-tion of instructional goals. For this reason the examination which serves the course best is that which has been planned, although not necessarily written, in advance of teaching, rather than one which is written two days before the typist sets a deadline for receipt of copy. A plan will rightly focus attention on the instructional goals to be covered, and the time spent in spelling them out is one of the best guarantees of developing simultaneously both a better course and a better test.

An early step in the test plan is to provide for coverage that is both adequate and in balance with the emphasis given to the instructional goals. Some teacher-selected body of materials and experiences, as well as those which the student elects, may have been utilized in the attainment of a particular objective. If the examination is to have "face validity," that is, incorporate material that the student considers fair (and there are important motiva-tional factors in this respect to heed), those materials should be sampled in accordance with the course emphasis. Sometimes an examination proves to have an imbalance in emphasis simply because the writer unconsciously yielded to the temptation to con-struct more questions on the use of the microscope, for example, than on the translation of physical phenomena to graphic form, because the one lent itself easily to test exercises. Actually much more time may have been spent on the latter objective. Therefore, to avoid the danger of this natural pitfall, there should be incor-porated in the plan an estimate of the number of questions that will be devoted to each phase of the program of studies.

An exact identification of the specific behaviors expected of the student will further refine the raw material from which the ques-tions later will be developed and provide specific test ideas. In this identification, the instructor will need to differentiate between content appropriate for grading purposes and content suitable only for evaluating the effectiveness of instruction. For example, while the development of appreciation for country may be a major goal of a course in American history, there are no simple means of measuring its attainment, since it is seldom possible to measure attitudes directly. Therefore, tests designed to get at attitudes or beliefs rarely, if ever, form an appropriate basis for grading students. Such efforts are likely to be more successful when they are divorced from grading.

Also, the itemizing of expected student behaviors frequently suggests the kinds of tasks or problems which seem most appropriate for measurement. It soon becomes apparent in the process of the work whether essay or objective questions will better serve the basic purposes of the test or whether an open-book examination or other project will provide a better measure. At this stage of planning, decisions regarding the types of questions to be used are quite in order. If they are made too early, however, thinking will be restricted to the outcomes which can be most easily measured by a certain form of question and equally important goals may be neglected altogether or, at best, poorly sampled.

Deciding on the kind of question to use

If the examination is to be a written one, and most are, a decision must be made on whether to choose a form that is objective, essay, or some combination of them.

In the objective-essay controversy, even the prejudiced instructor grants the objective-test form two advantages: it is simple to grade and it permits a much more comprehensive sampling of the course materials. While the experience of test builders indicates that it is possible to develop objective tests that do measure many complex abilities, the skeptical college instructor, reviewing his own student experiences, or thinking only in terms of some objective tests he has seen or written, questions this. He may thus believe that essay or discussion questions designed to elicit creative critical responses are preferable. But as he considers an essay approach he also recalls how he had to ponder his former instructors' meanings in test questions, and he also is aware of the tendency of his students to parrot his classroom discussions, or their readings, in such examinations.

Either approach then—objective or essay—may have disadvantages. Thus, in deciding the issue his best course is to examine the values and limitations of each and to consider which approach, or modification thereof, better serves the intrinsic purposes of his instructional goals.

Kinds of objective questions.—There is no need to belabor the reader here with descriptions of the common forms of objective test items. Ebel[3] provides such descriptions, states some of the cardinal principles in developing them, and also provides additional annotated sources of information on this subject. As Ebel points out, it has become increasingly clear from research findings that "such characteristic differences as may exist among item forms are of trivial consequence when compared with the extreme differences observed among items of the same form." Therein lies a warning that no form is particularly easy to prepare and that the task of "item writing" must be approached by the uninitiated with due respect for all the pitfalls.

There are many variations of the forms described by Ebel that may have greater appeal for the more advanced test writer or for those who are seeking test forms to utilize in measurement problems of more complex structure. Such persons may find it fruitful to review the *Taxonomy of Educational Objectives*.[4] In it will be found objective and essay forms that illustrate test questions whose aim is to measure both highly developed intellectual skills and the simpler results of instruction. These are arranged around an axis that includes the following instructional objectives:

A. Knowledge
  1. Of specifics
    a) Of terminology
    b) Of specific facts
  2. Of ways and means of dealing with specifics
    a) Of conventions
    b) Of trends and sequences
    c) Of classifications and categories
    d) Of criteria
    e) Of methodology
  3. Of universals and abstractions in a field
    a) Of principles and generalizations
    b) Of theories and structures
B. Intellectual abilities and skills
  1. Comprehension
  2. Translation
  3. Interpretation

B. Intellectual abilities and skills—*continued*
  4. Extrapolation
  5. Application
  6. Analysis
    a) Of elements
    b) Of relationships
    c) Of organizational principles
  7. Synthesis
    a) Production of a unique communication
    b) Production of a plan or a proposed set of operations
    c) Derivation of a set of abstract relations
  8. Evaluation
    a) Judgments in terms of internal evidence
    b) Judgments in terms of external criteria

[3] Robert L. Ebel, "Writing the Test Item," in *Educational Measurement*, pp. 193 ff. and 189.
[4] Benjamin S. Bloom and D. R. Krathwohl, *Taxonomy of Educational Objectives* (New York: Longmans, Green & Co., 1954). See Appendix.

There are other sources that might also be scanned for the suggestions they provide for achievement test forms. Most of these works will be cited in chapter 6 for their usefulness in other respects. The Dressel portfolio of science test items provides many interesting test forms, classified by objective being evaluated[5]; according to the *Taxonomy* mentioned above, the instruments developed in the evaluation program in the Eight-Year Study, albeit almost as well known for their scoring complexities as for their intrinsic merits, are described by Smith.[6] Instruments developed in the two American Council cooperative college studies in general education, one directed by Tyler (1942)[7] and one by Dressel (1954)[8] are described in some detail in the reports of those projects. The theory of the work-sample approach exemplified in the USAFI Tests of General Educational Development is described by Lindquist.[9]

The essay examination.—A good essay question provides for depth of response, and this and its influence on study are its most important assets. Essay questions must be as carefully planned as objective examinations; properly stated, questions can be used to estimate the student's ability to organize discussion of cause and effect relationships, or to evaluate conclusions, or to reveal insight in critical analysis.

But the essay question also has serious limitations. Intended to show how well the student can marshal and organize ideas—a skill considered to be of permanent value—it requires that this be

[5] Paul L. Dressel and Clarence H. Nelson, *Questions and Problems in Science: Test Item Folio No. 1* (Princeton, N.J.: Educational Testing Service, 1956).

[6] Eugene R. Smith, Ralph W. Tyler, and the Evaluation Staff, *Appraising and Recording Student Progress* (New York: McGraw-Hill Book Co., 1942).

[7] Four volumes report this work: Paul A. Brouwer, *Student Personnel Services in General Education;* Harold B. Dunkel, *General Education in the Humanities;* Albert William Levi, *General Education in the Social Studies;* and *Cooperation in General Education: A Final Report of the Executive Committee of the Cooperative Study in General Education.* All these volumes have been published by the American Council on Education, Washington, D.C.

[8] Paul L. Dressel and Lewis Mayhew, *General Education: Explorations in Education* (Washington: American Council on Education, 1954).

[9] E. F. Lindquist, "The Use of Tests in the Accreditation of Military Experience and in the Educational Placement of War Veterans," *Educational Record,* 25: 357–76, October 1944.

In addition to those mentioned, the reader may wish to examine other bibliographies on tests in instruction. A fairly recent one appears in: J. Raymond Gerberich, *Specimen Objective Test Items: A Guide to Achievement Test Construction* (New York: Longmans, Green & Co., 1956).

done in a quite unnatural situation. Seldom does a real problem require a written analysis "off the cuff" or within a two- or three-hour time limit, since in ordinary circumstances there is time for preliminary thinking or recourse to basic sources. Answering an essay question is more closely related to a group discussion where the individual is required, under immediate necessity, to give a penetrating oral analysis of a problem. Yet, though the essay question does have some relation to a natural situation, it serves even there less well than would a class discussion structured for the purpose.

The essay examination is time-consuming for the student, and the instructor finds it quite difficult to grade. He suspects his own impartiality and his grading criteria. Also, too frequently it suffers either from having too rigid boundaries or being so broad that the instructor's task of determining whether important objectives of instruction have been met becomes formidable, if not totally impossible.

Many essay questions do not actually measure what they are intended to measure. For example, a question may be intended to measure how well a student can organize and present ideas about a topic rather than to reveal the breadth of his information. If he happens to lack the segment of information on which the question hinges, he cannot answer, even though he does possess the ability to arrange ideas in a logical and well-organized way and could demonstrate this with other equally relevant segments not called for.

Some of the objections to difficulty of grading can be acceptably met if grading categories are well defined and if students are informed of them. Thus, if a question requests original illustrations of the application of a certain principle in physics, credit should not be given for the recounting of illustrations used by the instructor or provided in the text, no matter how accurate they may be. Methods of stabilizing the grading of essay examinations are suggested by Stalnaker.[10]

Special test material.—This brings us to a very important point:

[10] John M. Stalnaker, "The Essay Type of Examination," in *Educational Measurement*, p. 522. This chapter is worthy of review for its treatment of other aspects of the problem: potential measurement value, criticisms, facilitation of learning, and suggestions for improving the essay examination.

evaluation need not be limited to paper-and-pencil techniques. Often direct observation of performance is quite feasible and is more reliable than indirect measurement. Thus, in a laboratory course, it is more telling to observe whether the student can use the balance scales and other instruments than to have him write about them. If necessary, rating scales can be prepared specifically to identify his facility in the elements of each operation. In some courses special projects which call for original work may be the only valid way of evaluating certain kinds of achievement. For example, while courses in short story writing may provide background on the principles and techniques of creating short stories, their primary objective will be demonstrated only when the student writes an acceptable short story.

In constructing evaluation instruments the instructor should not feel confined to traditional media. The effectiveness of a test can be much enhanced by imaginative techniques. These may be difficult to control, but experience will help refine them. Botany classes can be sent out to the college campus to examine natural materials; graphs, art reproductions, stories of group interaction, and the like can be projected on the classroom screen; students can hear music, speeches, argument, foreign languages, literary productions, and the like recorded on tape; laboratory experiments in physics can be set in motion. These and similar media can provide the basic content or backdrop for testing—whether the tests be objective or essay—and, because they are more dramatic, can arouse student interest in the examination to a high level and thus motivate learning.

The open-book examination.—The open-book examination is a technique which can be adapted to evaluating certain kinds of results of course instruction. One of its major values is its approximation of real life problems for which it is more important to know the source of information and how to use it than to be able to recall it. In the same way that a writer refers to a grammar to solve a problem of syntax or usage, or an engineer refers to tables of constants or model problems to solve a mathematical problem, or a sociologist refers to a textbook on statistics to select the best method for analyzing his data, so also the instructor, in evaluating the student's ability to use sources skillfully, can devise problems that require reference to special sources. Naturally, the problem is the better if it requires integration and interpretation of materials rather than a pat answer from a book. It should also be complex enough to challenge the student and give an advantage to the one who has a command of his material in the sense that he knows his sources well and does not waste time searching at random for his information.

Review of test questions

It is seldom possible for one person to anticipate all the possible faulty interpretations that students make merely in trying to comprehend a test question. Any test, therefore, is likely to be improved if it is submitted to criticism before use. Sometimes a minor rewording will remove an ambiguity.

In preparing examinations for large courses that involve a number of instructors, the advantages of cooperative effort are most often realized. Not only can criticism of questions be obtained, but the sheer labor for the individual is reduced with the sharing of the task. In these courses and in courses taught by a staff rather than by an individual, it is normally advisable to introduce some element of control so that the several instructors will cover similar objectives. Cooperation in the common task can do much to weld the staff in refining objectives, selecting learning experiences, and improving teaching methods.

THE STATISTICAL ANALYSIS OF STUDENT RESPONSES

Statistical analyses of student responses to test questions help to disclose defects that have eluded the test writer and critics. Further, a careful examination of student responses is necessary to making judgments of the effectiveness of teaching. The basic purpose of analysis is to determine how the individual test questions function. For example, if the test is of the objective multiple-choice variety, it is useful to learn whether each of the wrong answers attracted at least some of the students who didn't know the right answer. Next, it is important to evaluate the extent to which individual test questions distinguish between students who have a grasp of the material represented by the test and those who have not mastered it; that is, does a test question discriminate between students earning high scores and students earning low scores?

Lastly, the difficulty of each question must be appraised: Were some questions so difficult that practically no student got them right? Were others so easy that virtually all students got them right? And how difficult was the test as a whole?

In the following sections, aspects of test analysis—distribution of responses, the discriminating power of items, and item difficulty —are discussed, and one method of analysis applicable even to groups as small as thirty or forty is presented. (However, it should be realized that for small groups the mathematical indices which the method provides will fluctuate more than with large groups. To obtain reasonably stable indications of item difficulty and discrimination on the basis of one test administration, it is recommended that analysis be based on 100, and preferably more, cases.)

Distribution of responses

The distribution of responses may be obtained as follows:

1. Place test papers in order of score from highest to lowest.

2. Select the one-third of the papers having the highest scores and the one-third of the papers having the lowest scores.

3. For each item in turn, tabulate the number of students in the top one-third (hereafter called the Highs) and the number of students in the bottom one-third (hereafter called the Lows) choosing each possible response to the item.

The tabulation might look like this for a four-choice multiple-choice item:

Item 38: The height of the tide is dependent, in part, upon the position of the moon in relation to the

A   planets
B   earth
C   plane of the ecliptic
D   sun

ITEM No.	GROUP	RESPONSES					
		Omitted	A	B*	C	D	Not Reached
38	Highs	5	23	50	10	12	
	Lows	8	35	10	42	3	2

* Correct answer.

It would appear from the figures above that item 38 discriminated quite well between Highs and Lows, since five times as many Highs as Lows responded correctly. Distractors A and C operated well, since both drew a large number who did not know the correct answer. Distractor D, however, bears study, as more Highs than Lows chose this as an answer. It is entirely possible that choice D may have been so worded that the Highs read into the distractor more than was intended, or the question, as in the case of the example given, may have had two correct answers. Thus it is that the distribution of responses often reveals ambiguities not readily apparent on preliminary consideration of the test and the responses.

Any objective-test item may be analyzed in the same way. Completion (fill-in-the-blank) questions may be analyzed by treating them as two-choice situations after scoring, as in the following example:

Item 25: In order to measure the specific gravity of battery acid, one would use a _____

ITEM No.	GROUP	RESPONSES			
		Omitted	Right	Wrong	Not Reached
25	Highs	2	20	8	
	Lows	8	8	12	2

The above analysis would indicate that the item apparently was not ambiguous, but it does not indicate either the quality or diversity of the acceptable and unacceptable responses.

Study of the number of students not reaching a question, that is, attempting neither it nor later questions, especially those near the end of the test, will provide information on what technicians call the "speededness" of a test. If the test is too highly speeded, a large proportion of the students will be unable to finish it. Although there are occasions when it is desirable to use tests that are highly speeded (for example, when measuring clerical speed and accuracy), for most purposes, especially for measuring educational achievement, it is desirable to have at least 90 percent of the students able to attempt every question.

Discriminating power of the item

Of prime importance is the question of how well an item discriminates between good and poor students. An index of discrimination of an item may be obtained simply by finding the difference between the number of Highs and Lows answering the item correctly;[11] this difference between the two sets of correct responses divided by the maximum possible difference gives the ratio to be used as the index of discrimination.

Although the desirable size of the index of discrimination will vary according to the purpose of the test, the range of ability within the group, the size of the sample, and the complexity of the material, it is generally thought that, for most achievement tests, indices that are negative or that range from 0 to .20 are low; those from .20 to .40 are average, while those of .40 or more are highly discriminating. Obviously, the minimum and maximum values of the discrimination index are minus 1.00 and plus 1.00, respectively.

In the kind of analyses presented above, the assumption has been made that the total score of the test is a true indicator of achievers and nonachievers. This assumption is safe if the test is both a good one and if it is the aim of all questions to reflect the same ability. Since classroom tests seldom measure one objective only, this is not a safe assumption for most achievement tests. In some analyses it is assumed that, while several objectives are represented in the questions, good students will be successful in all of them and poor students in none; this again is a questionable assumption. Unless further examination of the test items is made, either of these assumptions could lead to the incorrect discard of perfectly good questions which happen to exist in the test in a minority and therefore carry less weight in the total score; or they may similarly lead to the perpetuation of test items of a certain nature, not necessarily most desirable, because they happen to be present in the test in great majority and therefore contribute

[11] This method was proposed by Robert L. Ebel. Details of the method and the assumptions involved are discussed by Ebel in "Procedures for the Analysis of Classroom Tests," *Educational and Psychological Measurement,* **14:** 352–63, 1954. Methods utilized by other technicians are described by Frederick B. Davis in *Educational Measurement,* pp. 266 ff.

inordinately to the total score which becomes the criterion for good and poor students.

Therefore, in tests where separate objectives are represented, it is advisable either to obtain separate criterion scores for each objective represented or to establish a criterion for good and poor students by using an outside criterion, such as teacher estimates of students who have or have not demonstrated the ability.

Difficulty of an item

Knowing the difficulty of an item is of great value in the future construction of tests. Item difficulty can readily be calculated from the same data obtained for determining the distribution of responses for the distractors or for calculating the discrimination index. One of the simplest and most usable indices of difficulty is the percentage of students in the total group who answered the item correctly.

If the purpose of the test is to differentiate among the students, it is obviously useless to include items that all students get right or that all students miss since these items make no differentiations. Generally, items in the middle range of difficulty provide the best differentiation. For some purposes, however, it is desirable to have most students get all, or almost all, of the questions right. This is true, for example, whenever it is desirable to learn how many students have reached a given level of proficiency in any area. Some diagnostic tests utilize this approach. Instructors often use some easy, some average, and some difficult items in constructing a test in order to provide an opportunity for both good and poor students to show what they know.

As useful as an item analysis is, it seldom provides a direct indication of the value of a test question. An item may produce unfavorable statistics because it was poorly worded or has two correct answers; revision of the question can correct such deficiencies. In other instances, the fault may lie with the learning or the instruction; for example, a particular point being tested may not have been adequately covered in class or in the text.

A test can show good item statistics simply because it wrongly favored the study emphases of a relatively few students. If approximately a third of a class emphasized a particular chapter in their study because they guessed it to be the instructor's field of specialty, those students would be high performers in the test and item statistics would be spuriously good; this would not mean the test was good, especially if it was supposed to be representative of a unit of work that covered, say, six chapters.

Item analyses, if properly interpreted by the instructor, can indicate the quality of his examination effort, suggest areas where learning has been poor, and help determine whether there are individuals of the class who require remedial work. Item analyses, however, are neither infallible nor completely informative: they never disclose directly how the individual student reacts to the particular questions. Thus, sometimes, item analyses need to be supplemented by interviews or by class discussion of questions to elicit a deeper and more exact reflection of student thinking. It may be found, for example, that students answer the questions correctly for the wrong reasons, or that a question which was intended to require primarily only factual recall elicits from the student complex rational thinking that involves much more than factual recall. This "thinking out loud" with students is profitable to both instructor and students.

5. The Use of Tests in Educational Counseling

FROM THE EARLIER DISCUSSIONS OF TESTS FOR ADMISSIONS AND PLACE-
ment purposes, the reader will see that essentially tests used for
those purposes also serve educational counseling functions. The
present chapter is concerned with some additional uses of scholastic aptitude and achievement test data by both faculty counselors
and administrative personnel in charge of college guidance activities. While other types of instruments and techniques will be cited
as important aspects of the counseling process, they will not be
discussed in detail. Also omitted are measures of nonintellectual
factors because (a) they have not yet been developed to the level
of technical excellence and ease of administration comparable to
that of measures of scholastic aptitude and achievement, and (b)
their use requires training and experience so specialized that a
limited description would fail to define their proper application
in good clinical counseling. The discussion here will be of problems and techniques more generally useful to the nonspecialist.

DETERMINING COUNSELING NEEDS

Counseling often takes place on an informal and part-time basis.
Admissions officers, for example, frequently advise prospective students (and their parents) regarding their chances of success at a
given college. Members of the general administrative staff and
department heads answer many queries concerning course requirements, programs of study, and so on. Faculty members, in their
capacities both as advisers and teachers, help students avoid irreg-
ularities in course sequences, work with them in developing suitable attitudes toward study, and aid them in seeing the relationship between their studies and their needs. Counseling also occurs
directly in classroom instruction, particularly in courses designed
to influence attitudes, with the skillful instructor stimulating the

student to assume responsibility for raising questions that perplex him so that they may receive specific attention; the relationship so engendered carries over in their individual contacts outside the classroom.

Because the counseling function is spread among so many persons, there is a danger that some serious problems may not be recognized and that some students will, therefore, fail to receive adequate help. This danger can be minimized if a college evolves a clearly defined point of view toward its responsibilities for providing specific kinds of guidance services and when the nature of those services becomes understood by all members of the college community. Therefore, a college that is initiating or expanding counseling services must give serious attention to assessing the nature and scope of student problems on its campus and then determine what it can and should do in counseling.

Studying the causes of student difficulties

Although no single approach to the appraisal of college counseling needs will cover all contingencies, the illustration of a hypothetical college which is trying to identify the causes of academic failure among freshmen will set forth a number of basic principles.

Let us assume that at College X, despite careful selection and placement procedures, academic failure among freshmen is alarmingly frequent. Some faculty members attribute this to the poor study habits of the students; others, to their lack of preparation in tool subjects; still others, to adjustment problems stemming from the excitement of living away from home; and there are those who maintain that the general caliber of the student body is not equal to the curriculum. A systematic review of the data on hand—secondary school records, aptitude and placement test data, and certain other additional data—may serve to identify one or more causes of freshman difficulties. To begin with, the college may review the class admissions and placement data and compare them with similar information for previous classes and may find that the class as a whole is of about the same caliber as recent entering classes.

It might then be advisable to examine the relationship between the various data and actual failure: it may be found that, by and large, the students with the poorest admission and placement data are having the most trouble. But the relationship probably will not be clear-cut, for some will be found to be doing well, and some of the better students, failing. A closer look at the backgrounds of the failing students may indicate that some of them had had problems of personal-social adjustment while they were still in high school, which might be affecting their work now. But again this will not be true for all.

Although the review thus far has yielded some information on possible causes of failure that might have been expected for some students, it by no means has accounted for enough cases to satisfy the inquiry. Therefore, several other approaches might be revealing. The courses failed might be reviewed to determine if failures are confined to one course. Freshman faculty advisers might be asked to report any personal-social adjustment problems of their advisees, and the students might be asked to complete a study habits inventory and a personal-social problems check list.

With this additional information, the college can further narrow down its study of freshman failures, getting at specific reasons for, say, a high proportion of failures in physics. It may well be that the students do not have sufficient skill in mathematics to handle the material as it is taught, despite satisfactory scores on the mathematics test. A further inspection of the test may indicate that it does not include some of the skills and abilities which the physics instructors are taking for granted. Similarly, failures in other courses, and the extent to which study habits or personal problems really are contributing to failing grades, may be examined.

When as much information as is thought to be available has been accumulated on the matter of freshman failures, College X must next face the problem of what to do to remedy the situation. What can and will be done will depend in part upon its academic traditions and philosophy and in part upon what is administratively feasible in terms of staff and budget.

There may be the feeling that all the college can hope to do is attack the problem on a group basis by (1) selecting a more appropriate mathematics placement test, (2) establishing a special non-credit mathematics course for students making low scores, and (3) utilizing a special period in the first weeks of the semester for intensive training in effective study habits for the deficient group. Any organized work with individual students, especially those who appear to have adjustment problems, it may be decided, will have to wait until the college can afford additional staff. Or, it may be thought essential, in addition to these administrative and instructional changes, to begin as soon as possible to work with individuals, and the college may therefore immediately secure the services of a person trained in counseling. It may then institute an in-service training program for those members of the instructional staff who seem most interested in and capable of handling guidance problems, and schedule interviews so that entering students may review the possible or actual difficulties facing them and the courses of action that might be adopted to circumvent or correct them.

This illustration, though largely hypothetical and by no means universal in its application, demonstrates several points: the role of tests in a survey of remedial and counseling needs; the supplementary nature of test data in surveys of group and individual problems; the choice of the instruments appropriate to the problem or problems being investigated; the use of data from other institutional programs for surveys or for individual counseling needs; the values of local, as well as published, normative data; the possible contributions of group surveys in the identification of problems for administrative planning purposes; and the choice of follow-up action that is appropriate to local conditions.

Defining categories of students who should be counseled

The establishment of the categories of counseling can be approached in several different ways. One way is to establish them in terms of particular kinds of educational, vocational, or personal problems that students experience. Thus, in the example just cited, the college identified such problems as academic deficiencies, poor study habits, adjustment problems, and so on, as factors which contributed to freshman failures. In another sense, however, it established a working category in terms of academic levels. It identified freshman students as a group that might need special assistance. This establishment of categories in terms of academic levels can often form a practical basis for helping students with their problems, since each different period in a student's career brings somewhat different stresses and strains which may be alleviated by providing some kind of systematic counseling.

The establishment of functional categories may be considered a longitudinal dimension for the organization of guidance services. The second approach may be considered a horizontal dimension for the establishment of counseling activities. Neither dimension is mutually exclusive. Obviously, sophomores as well as entering freshmen may have faulty attitudes which interfere with effective academic performance, and freshmen as well as seniors may be concerned about their future vocational plans. Just as the two dimensions are not mutually exclusive, it is almost equally certain that no one college would wish to establish its counseling activities solely in terms of one rather than another dimension. Nevertheless, viewing counseling problems first in one way and then in another can be helpful in planning for and working toward an appropriate balance between counseling students who are chosen according to administratively defined categories and counseling individual students who, upon their own initiative, seek special help.

A VIEW OF COUNSELING PROBLEMS IN TERMS OF ACADEMIC LEVELS

Since the major focus of this discussion is upon the use of scholastic aptitude and achievement data in educational counseling, and specifically upon the use of data from tests administered on an institution-wide basis, it may be helpful first to view counseling problems in terms of horizontal categories. Within each category problems on other dimensions will appear, but primary attention will be given to the kinds of educational problems which most often make their appearance at given levels.

The prospective student level

A college cannot hope to provide extensive counseling services for all prospective students, but some counseling is eminently desirable. It gives both the applicant and the college an opportunity to relate his qualifications, ultimate career goals, and other interests to the academic and social program that the college offers. Both the college and the applicant will benefit from this review. The college can be more certain of the wisdom of its ultimate decision in accepting or rejecting the applicant; and for the applicant, whether he is accepted or rejected, it can be an important step in self-knowledge. He may be genuinely puzzled about the demands of college life, uncertain of his own ability to compete in a more selective academic environment, unsure of his future vocational plans, and so forth. If the data collected in the admissions process are wisely used, he can be assisted to a better understanding of his problems and adjustments.

The student's secondary school record will not be new to him. What will be new is how his record compares with that of other freshmen who have attended different secondary schools and with those of older successful students in the college. In these terms, is his record good, poor, or mediocre, and what does it mean in terms of his probable success if he is admitted? Even if no other data were available, this review of the student's school record would be beneficial to him.

In many instances, however, additional information is available. Many colleges require tests as one of their admissions procedures —for example, a test like the College Board Scholastic Aptitude Test or the School and College Ability Tests, which yield verbal and quantitative scores, or a test like the Ohio State University Intelligence Test, which yields a total score based largely on verbal material. Whatever the test, the college usually will have studied the relationship of its scores, and other admissions data, to success on its campus. Thus, the admissions staff can help the applicant determine his chances of success and, further, consider the programs for which he is best fitted, if indeed he is generally prepared for that college. No final decisions concerning his academic program are made at this point, for if he is accepted, he will likely review this information, and perhaps additional data, with a freshman adviser. But in the meantime, he and his parents can be giving some thought to his future plans. Perhaps he has entertained thoughts of studying engineering without having a realistic picture of the required background and skills. If he learns that his preparation and ability in mathematics are only minimal for engineering, and learns more about other options available to him, he may decide to follow some other program. Or, he may decide to give engineering a try, but at least he knows in advance that he may run into trouble.

Then there is the applicant who does not meet the standards of admission to the four-year degree-granting programs of the college. He may be guided into a two-year program at this college or some other institution. Frequently, such a suggestion will require the student and his parents to reconsider his plans both in terms of accepting such a solution or in thinking about vocational areas for which two-year programs offer preparation.

Many colleges also include one or more achievement tests in their admissions requirements. Like scholastic ability tests, scores on these instruments, when they are related to college success generally and to success in specific programs, yield data to help the candidate appraise the adequacy of his academic preparation for the demands of a particular college. If he is weak in an area which is considered prerequisite for a particular program, he may be helped to realize that special tutoring over the summer can make a significant difference in his chances of success the following year. Conceivably, additional data from other tests will be needed before the student is in a position to plan finally, but at least a step in the direction of greater self-knowledge will have been taken.

Entering freshmen

Freshmen require assistance with a host of problems. Academically, they need help in selecting courses of study which are compatible with their abilities, preparation, and interests. They need help in scheduling their programs and in relating their studies to their future college work and career plans. They also need to become acquainted with campus regulations, traditions, student mores, extracurricular activities and social clubs, and, more important, they may need help in choosing among them.

Obviously not all questions which puzzle freshmen can be answered by reference to test data, but many can, because information on the student's intellectual qualifications is crucial in making intelligent decisions about the courses he will select and the general regimen that he will follow. Therefore, whenever possible, test data should be made easily available to the faculty advisers and counselors who are guiding freshmen.

The kinds of tests incorporated in the freshman guidance program should, to a large extent, depend not only on the courses of study and the breadth and scope of guidance services the college offers, but also on the extent to which tests are used for admissions and/or course placement purposes. If the college does not employ tests for either purpose, it is obvious that the tests used to help freshmen should include a measure of general ability and tests of achievement of those skills or basic understandings which are considered prerequisite to required college courses. But, if a scholastic aptitude test has been used in admissions and if placement is based in part upon test performance, considerable information is already available, and time which would otherwise be devoted to testing may be devoted to the counseling process itself or to the administration of supplementary tests.

What additional tests the college will find helpful will depend, in part, upon the scope and complexities of its curricular offerings and policies and the comprehensiveness of its guidance services. Many colleges, especially those offering programs oriented toward specific vocations, incorporate in their freshman testing programs tests of special abilities (music, mechanical, and art aptitude) and they administer them, if not to all students, at least to those who wish to register in these special programs. Some colleges administer measures of interest and study habits. Still others may administer a group test intended to measure personal and social traits in order to identify those students who show signs of needing special help. Students so identified will then be encouraged to meet with counselors who are particularly well qualified to provide personal counseling. In a majority of situations, however, the information which will be of most potential value to the adviser and the student will be that which provides information on the student's academic skills and interests.

An obviously gifted student may be encouraged to take a more difficult program. If the college provides opportunities for gifted freshmen to by-pass prerequisites, these will be explained to him, and he may be encouraged to seek exemption in areas in which he appears strong. If the student's achievement record as well as his scholastic aptitude scores show he is marginally prepared, the wisdom of taking a minimum program will be discussed with him. If the college offers remedial programs on a voluntary basis, he will be encouraged to enroll in them if it is probable that he will benefit from the special work.

Scholastic aptitude and achievement test data, then, combined with high school grades, statements of the student's interests, and records of previous school and work activities, when used with insight into and understanding of the student that the counselor gains in the interview, provide a wealth of information to the counselor in aiding the student.

Sophomores

Students nearing the end of their sophomore year have presumably reached the point where they will make a decision about their fields of major concentration. Some of them, indeed, came to college with their minds already made up, and all of their work thus far, barring basic general requirements, has been related to their choices. Others have come with relatively clear goals but have found the going harder than they expected. Thus, we may find hopeful mathematics majors facing almost certain failure if they continue mathematics, yet uncertain about the choice of another major. Other students find themselves entertaining two or more choices which appear equally attractive. Or some students simply do not appear to be especially interested in any particular field. All except the students who are performing successfully in areas related to their proposed major require some help in thinking through the decisions they must ultimately make. And almost all need help in relating their educational choices to their future vocational plans. What data will be helpful to them and their counselors?

Obviously, the student's academic record for his first two years of college will be an important piece of evidence to review. So also will be scores on the various tests he has taken prior to and after entrance. In addition, qualitative data about his college activities, his personal relationships with faculty and other students, social and career aspirations, and so forth, will also enter the picture and lend nuances of meaning to the data at hand.

The student who has a record of failures and barely passing grades as well as low achievement scores may appear to be a clear-cut case to the counselor—he should not continue in a college where the enrollment becomes more selective and the competition greater each year. Yet the case is far from clear-cut if the student's general average is just high enough to permit him to stay and if he wishes to stay. He may have just enough determination to make the grade if he remains at college, or he may be able to make better grades in his major subject, and for this reason alone one would be reluctant to advise categorically that he leave. But the cards do seem stacked against him, and his situation should be made clear to him with all of the tact and understanding that can be brought to bear in the situation and, whenever possible, alternate courses of action suggested.

The student with an erratic performance record frequently presents an easier problem. Often his test scores will corroborate his academic record as far as his strong and weak points are concerned. They may add little more than this, although at times they may indicate that an able student has antipathies to subject, teacher, or teaching methods. In any event, scores are often helpful in confirming the student's choice of major field, since in most cases a student with a particular area of competence will tend to choose a major field that is compatible with his strength.

Even though the test record may at first glance seem only to substantiate the academic record, it can on occasion be even more discriminating, for while the academic record shows the student how he stands in relation to other students at his college, the test record shows how he stands in comparison with a larger group of college students and thus presents him with a better picture of his strong and weak points. This can be especially valuable if the student is contemplating a professional choice which may require graduate training or further academic competition.

The student, too, whose record shows that he can succeed at almost anything to which he turns can, and often does, confound the counselor. If he has already decided to major in history, there seems to be little advantage in showing him that he could be equally successful in English or American literature; or if he has chosen physics, there is no point in indicating that he could do just as well in chemistry or mathematics. There may be need though to review his vocational plans to see if another, though perhaps related, area will better serve his plans.

The student who appears to have no outstanding interest in any one field can be most puzzling. Perhaps he is competent in the quantitative or verbal areas, but has no clear preference for a specific field within either category and as yet has only the most tentative ambitions. Here the counselor will have to muster all the information he can about the student's major interests through a review of his activities, likes, and dislikes and through the results of an interest inventory in order to help him identify the possible courses open to him. Frequently, for such a student, summer or other work experience helps to develop his attitudes and to sharpen his thinking.

Juniors

Unlike entering freshmen, juniors are not adjusting to college; unlike sophomores, they are not reaching that crucial point where they must choose their major programs, and unlike seniors, they are not yet ready to leave their ivory towers. As a result, they are usually exempt, by and large, from any institution-wide testing programs designed to aid in their selection, placement, or guidance, or designed to evaluate the extent to which certain institutional objectives are being achieved. Nevertheless, though we may ignore the educational needs of juniors as a class, individual juniors may need help. A junior occasionally finds that either because of academic difficulties or a change in career plans, he has made a mistake in choosing his major field. Can his program be changed without serious loss of time or credits? Another finds that he now needs a course which he thought he did not need. Can it be worked into his schedule? Whatever the problems juniors bring to their advisers or counselors, some of them at least will be similar to those that beset harassed sophomores or freshmen. Similar types of evidence and information will be needed to help them.

Seniors

Some seniors run into academic problems which, unless properly met, threaten their chances of graduating with their class. But most seniors, if perplexed at all, could have their problems summarized in the question: What do I do after graduation? For this group, then, the problems are more likely to fall into the realm of career rather than educational counseling and thus fall outside the limits of the discussion here. Nevertheless, it may be useful to review briefly some of the problems they face and to suggest a few ways in which they may be helped even though specially trained counselors are not available.

Most seniors are attempting to make their first job choices. A number of them may want considerable help in making this choice or may at least want some assurance that their selections are wise ones. Even the engineering graduate who sees a number of industrial recruiting officers needs help in deciding whether he is better suited for sales or production engineering, for design or research. And if he has settled that question, he may have specific points to resolve regarding the relative merits of a large or small company and other similar questions. For those whose college training has been less oriented toward a particular professional area, the problem of a first job choice can be difficult. Personnel officers are not clamoring at their doors; they must do the knocking. When and how should they do this? This can be an irksome and difficult problem for the senior even if he has decided that he prefers insurance to accounting or advertising to banking.

More difficult are the problems facing the senior who has only a vague notion of what he would like to do, or perhaps only clear ideas of what he would not like to do. And still more difficult perhaps are the problems facing the would-be lawyer or doctor who has not been accepted in a professional school and must therefore make an alternate career choice, clearly not his first preference.

All these students need information—information on occupational groupings and the training necessary for beginning careers, on specific types of jobs within occupational families, and on how to write letters of application and how to approach the job interview. Much of the counseling at this stage will therefore be directed to showing these students how they may obtain the information they need. A certain amount of it will be aimed at reassurance and may involve the review of the student's college record—grades, test scores, and activities. Some of it will be directed toward his developing greater self-knowledge and helping him to develop a problem-solving approach to the choice of a career. Again, this

may involve a review of all the evidence available and the necessity, perhaps, of collecting additional data, such as scores on an
interest measure, to help him correlate what he likes to do with
what he is able to do and with what the working world requires.

A VIEW OF SOME SPECIAL TYPES OF COUNSELING PROBLEMS

It may now be helpful to take a somewhat closer look at several
problems which may appear at any of the academic levels, but
which are particularly critical as students begin their college work.

Students with academic deficiencies

Even when selection is highly competitive, there will be some
students who in terms of both general ability and academic preparation are marginally prepared for a particular college. In colleges
with lower admissions requirements, there is likely to be an even
greater number of such students, many of whom face almost certain failure unless they receive help, and many others, unfortunately, who may fail even if they do receive help. It is important
then for colleges to identify these students early and especially to
distinguish between those who may profit from special help and
those who should be guided toward other types of training.

The weakest students will be those who fall at the low extreme
of their classes according to all the data available—test scores and
academic records. For some of these students, remedial work in
such tool subjects as reading and mathematics may be beneficial,
since lack of skill in these areas may have been the cause of lack
of success in content subjects and of poor performance on aptitude
tests. Unfortunately, however, this will not always be the case. Students performing at a relatively low level in the basic skills may
actually be performing at a level commensurate with their general ability. In such cases, remedial programs will not usually
bring about any significant improvement in basic skills. However,
since it is rarely clear which came first, the low ability or the poor
skills, it is often desirable to give such students an opportunity
to obtain special help. At the same time, they must be helped to
realize that they may face academic difficulties and that, perhaps,
vocational training will be more compatible with their abilities.

In other cases, there is considerable likelihood that students will benefit from remedial work if they apply themselves seriously. Such students will demonstrate a weakness in a basic skill area while performing at a relatively higher level on a measure of scholastic aptitude. Students who show this pattern in their test and academic performance often have the necessary general ability, but have failed to master some of the basic skills for one reason or another. If helped early in their college careers, they can often compensate for their earlier lack of proficiency and do creditable college work.

Other problems of academic deficiency will occur as students progress through college. Some of these will be serious enough to jeopardize their chances of graduation, and efforts should be made to understand the possible causes. Is the student working at his optimum level? If this is the case, should he attempt to continue or should he be guided toward considering alternative courses of action? If his academic and test records indicate that he should be able to perform at a satisfactory level, what factors may be contributing to his unsatisfactory performance in one or more courses? Is he in a field which holds little of interest to him? Does he have poor study habits? Is he preoccupied with personal problems that vitiate his efforts to concentrate? Is he too busy with campus activities, work, community, or social activities to organize his time efficiently? Is he physically well? Tests, of course, will not supply the answers to all of these questions, but they will help the counselor and the student reach the conclusion that he is not doing as well as he is capable of doing. With this established, one usually needs to look elsewhere to establish the real causes of difficulty.

Gifted students

The need to counsel gifted students is likely to appear less urgent on most campuses than the need to counsel the academically weak. Unless the gifted student is so little challenged that he is unable to channel his abilities effectively or has personal problems which interfere with his ability to concentrate, the gifted student is likely to do acceptable, although not always outstanding, work. He does not, therefore, tend to come to the attention of the faculty or administration as one who needs help. But because of his potential as a prospective high-level professional person or technician, he should have all of the help possible in planning a challenging program of study.

There are two aspects to this problem. One is that of identification. Who are the gifted students, and how do we know whether or not they are performing below their capacities? Test data and the other kinds of evidence we have discussed will be helpful here. High test scores and only average or slightly above average academic grades will indicate that a particular student needs encouragement, assistance, or a forthright "talking to." High test scores and a good academic record may indicate that a student is working near his capacity; on the other hand, it may not. We have no way of knowing whether he could do better until he has attempted more difficult work.

This brings us to the second aspect of the problem. What can be done to provide the gifted student with greater challenge? Here it will be largely a matter of what a particular college can provide in the way of added intellectual stimulation for the very able. One question concerns the number of such students on the campus. Does a very bright student have any peers, or does he stand alone? What training and preparation do individual faculty members have that can contribute to education of the gifted? Are there instructors in each department who are themselves strong enough to offer the challenge these students need? Are the local library research facilities adequate for stimulating independent study and research? And so, question can be piled upon question in determining whether a particular campus is able or willing, in terms of its traditions and purposes, to provide the kind of intellectual environment which will meet the needs of the most gifted. Assuming that a given college can meet the challenge of the gifted student, provision must then be made to identify him when he enters and to provide for periodic review of his performance and for guidance throughout his college years.

Special cases

Colleges may find that students from various ethnic or religious minority groups present more personal and/or social problems than they do academic or vocational problems. Some, especially those from noncollege oriented backgrounds, may have—instead of, or in addition to, personal problems—academic problems which stem from a cultural impoverishment of their homes and environments. They may lack the breadth of intellectual associations to make much of their college work meaningful and enjoyable. They may be openly hostile to certain kinds of ideas in course work or simply indifferent to the best efforts of some of their professors. Others may be sincerely interested in making up their deficiencies, but find the going difficult. Both types of students present educational counseling problems and will need help in scheduling their course work so that they will experience success and have their intellectual curiosities aroused.

In a category by themselves, perhaps, will be students from other countries who, in addition to having come from different cultural backgrounds, will have come from school situations which differ markedly from those in the United States. The content and sequence of course work may have been quite different. Some will be better prepared in certain subjects than many of our students; in other areas, they will be less well prepared. How can their academic preparation be evaluated so that they may be placed in courses which offer both success and challenge?

For these students, as well as for some of the subgroups within our own culture, tests are likely to be less helpful than they are with the average white middle-class college student. We can be sure in most cases that these students are at least as good as their test scores indicate, and in many cases there is every likelihood that they are better. But how much better is a question which most colleges are unable to answer either for groups or for individuals, simply because they may not have sufficient data on such groups of students to know what kinds of school records and test scores best separate the academic successes from the academic failures. Only a history, compiled over a long period of time, will help to build up information which can be used to predict the likelihood of success for these students.

Many otherwise bright and well-educated foreign students will have initial difficulties with their work in American colleges because of insufficient knowledge of English or even unfamiliarity with classroom teacher-student relationships. Whatever the problems, they need special help in making satisfactory social adjustments to the mores of American college students while at the same time retaining their own national individuality so that they do not become alienated in thought and custom from their own people.

There are, of course, other categories of students who need special counseling if they are to make satisfactory adjustments in college and in later life. They may be students with severe physical handicaps who need special educational and vocational help as well as personal assistance if they are to learn to lead lives that are optimally useful and happy. Others are students with emotional disturbances. Most of these problems, however, fall within the realm of personal counseling.

UTILIZING TEST AND OTHER DATA IN EDUCATIONAL COUNSELING

In the preceding sections mention has been made of the role that scholastic aptitude and achievement data can play in dealing with the various types of educational and vocational problems that college students face. The full value of the data used in the counseling process, however, will be realized only if they are interpreted within frames of reference which have meaning for the problems being studied. This is true for all the data being used, but presents special problems when test scores are being employed.

The use of published norms

At the secondary school level, when a counselor presumes to help a youngster in his educational planning it is often essential to go beyond the local school and think of all secondary school students, since soon he will be competing with others outside his own school. Published norms will be necessary to make the comparison.

At the college level a relatively small proportion of the students will be competing scholastically with students outside their own institution, but some will be considering a transfer to another college and others will be considering choice of a graduate school. For these groups, norms based on a larger number of college students will be very useful. However, norms of this type have limited usefulness in other aspects of educational guidance. In many cases, they are totally unnecessary except to answer a student's legitimate interest in knowing how he compares with college students in general, that is, how he compares with the students who happen to be in the norms population. Also, in a few situations, where a college has not yet been able to establish its own norms, published norms may serve as a point of departure in arriving at decisions that would be difficult without some comparative information.

The value of local norms

By and large, the use of tests in educational counseling is a matter of prediction, and prediction involves criteria of success in a well-defined situation. Thus, at the college level when a student is planning his educational program, he must do so in terms of the demands of a particular college and in terms of local competition. For problems of this type, local norms will be of primary importance. It does not matter whether the student stands at the 65th percentile on the published norms on a scholastic aptitude test if on local norms he stands at the 30th percentile. Regardless of whether he is about average or slightly above average in general ability as far as college students in general are concerned, on this campus he is in the lower third and in all likelihood will find the going difficult unless he develops excellent study habits and applies himself diligently. So also in achievement areas he is better able to see how his academic preparation compares with that of other students.

To be of most value, however, local norms must be carefully compiled. In small colleges this may often mean waiting two or three years, sometimes longer, so that a sufficient number of students will be represented in the norms to make them dependable. Thereafter, they should be checked not only when there are good reasons to expect marked changes in the characteristics of the student body but at periodic intervals, since gradual and unnoticed changes in the enrollment may be taking place.[1]

A college can use local data in educational counseling in another important way. Because the norms, usually percentiles, for all the tests are based on the same student population, comparisons across tests can be made. While publisher's norms can sometimes be used for comparison purposes, they offer the serious limitation that it must be assumed that the norms are based on populations that are very similar to, if not the same as, the college's student

---

[1] Methods for developing local tables of percentile ranks are presented in almost any standard statistics text.

population. Use of local norms obviates any assumption concerning comparability.[2]

THE NATURE AND SUCCESS OF COUNSELING SERVICES

The nature of the counseling services in any institution reflects the educational and organizational philosophy of the institution's guiding personalities—their concept of what counseling can and should do; their estimate of the support for counseling that is administratively defensible in terms of money, staff, and facilities; the ability level of the student body, the level of scholastic and personal preparation for college, and other pertinent characteristics.

Effective counseling services, in which the roles of administrative counselors, faculty counselors, student personnel counselors, and specialized testing and guidance counselors are well coordinated, requires careful planning, careful staffing, and continued adaptation to the evolving needs of the student body. These needs change as the proportion of veterans changes; as the proportion of students with college-educated parents changes; as the ability level and level of preparation of the students change; as the economic prosperity of the students, of their home communities, and of the college community changes; as the ratio of male to female students changes; as the tendency of students to marry during college years changes; and so forth.

The success of counseling services depends primarily upon the human and professional qualities of the staff and their willingness to put their hearts as well as their minds to the task of doing what is best for the long-range development of each student, yet remain sensitive to administrative necessities. Students will be the first to recognize sympathetic and understanding counseling. Of equal importance to the success of counseling is whole-hearted administrative support, which will ensure that these services are realistically adapted to the educational objectives and needs of the institution.

[2] Some batteries of published tests provide for comparability. If the college is using such a battery, it need not develop local norms before plotting student scores on profile charts. In many instances, however, it will be found helpful to substitute local norms for published data, or to superimpose local norms on the published data.

6. The Use of Tests in General Institutional Evaluation

IN THE LAST SEVERAL CHAPTERS THOSE APPLICATIONS OF TESTING related chiefly to the day-to-day operation of the educational institution have been considered. For the most part, they have concerned provisions for the welfare of students—the initial screening to determine their fitness for particular programs, their guidance after admission, the improvement of their courses, and the evaluation of their progress in courses and of their interest in general.

In addition, test results can supply policy-making groups of an institution with some of the evidence needed to reach decisions for the collective good. Scores can also contribute information when an institution wishes to take an over-all view of its educational enterprise in order to identify procedures that seem to be accomplishing the purpose for which they were created and procedures that are in need of modification.

On those occasions when tests are selected or constructed for measuring various instructional objectives, they often become the focal point of a dynamic process of exchange of opinion and thus serve to get issues described, reviewed, and clarified for the benefit of all concerned.

The present discussion considers the design of the more common institutional self-surveys that employ tests as one means for evaluating attainment of major educational goals and needs. A comprehensive institutional evaluation will necessarily be long-range in plan and will continue over several years, since even the first step necessitates a complete description by the instructional staff of the outcomes expected.[1] The preparation of the descrip-

---

[1] For a list of the kinds of questions faced at the outset in an evaluation of general education, for example, see Paul L. Dressel, "Evaluation Procedures for General Education Objectives," *Educational Record,* **31**: 97–122, April 1950; or see Paul L. Dressel and Lewis Mayhew, *General Education: Explorations in Evaluation* (Washington: American Council on Education, 1954), p. 21.

tions takes time, and even more time is required for the actual outcomes to be demonstrated by the instructed. The analysis begins with the formulation of a complete blueprint of the major outcomes that are expected from all the units of the program. From among the outcomes must be selected those which reflect the chief concerns of the institution. Sometimes the selection may be of a particular unit of instruction and therefore the evaluation limited to a narrow sector of the institution's program. This would be the case if it were decided, for example, to examine the institution's offerings in modern languages. On the other hand, some objective of the institution which is much more pervasive in its effects might be selected; under these circumstances, the evaluation endeavor can become quite complex.

The most logical and defensible approach to the selection of objectives for evaluation is that which emphasizes the attainment of outcomes considered to be most important in every unit of the educational process, or perhaps most important to all units collectively; however, circumstances of expediency (time, budget, personnel, available instruments, and the like) usually dictate other criteria of selection. Selection of objectives to be appraised at a particular time may then be related (*a*) to some one unit, say, to the area of humanities, with plans to consider other divisions being held in abeyance; or (*b*) to a particular level, say the sophomore class, since the dropout rate at that level indicates that the two-year product is representative of the institution and it may be desirable to know what he is like; or (*c*) to a sophomore class, to determine whether the background and skills required for continuation are being mastered; or (*d*) to a particular instructional area, to demonstrate that it is a weak link in achieving a sought-after integration; or (*e*) to areas in which tests have been published. (If the institution does have resources for developing tests and, thus, greater flexibility in devising instruments to measure outcomes, it is best to confine the test construction to measures that supplement, rather than duplicate, published tests.)

While the above list is obviously incomplete, it does list some of the choices an institution may make instead of attempting to measure many objectives with less effectiveness. At the same time, an over-all blueprint and long-range plan will serve to place the selected portions in proper perspective so that they will not receive undue emphasis merely because they are temporarily identified for study.

THE APPRAISAL OF GENERAL VERSUS SPECIALIZED OUTCOMES OF EDUCATION

Most American colleges offer a two-pronged program, endeavoring, on the one hand, to impart general knowledge and skills to students through traditional liberal arts courses and/or programs of general studies and, on the other, to develop proficiency in a more specialized field of knowledge. Although there are differing patterns for accomplishing these objectives, it is now common to stress the first purpose in the first two years of instruction and the second in the last two years. Regardless of the pattern of courses and programs adopted, the use of some measure of degree of attainment offers a starting point for the evaluation of the college's educational process.

When the general goals and purposes have been defined in terms sufficiently concrete to be identifiable for evaluation, it is then possible to determine what evidence will reveal progress toward attainment. For evidence of progress toward some goals, records may provide the most appropriate information; for others, special observations by the faculty may be required; and so forth. It is in the measurement of academic accomplishments that well-conceived and well-constructed tests may be of special assistance. Where course objectives and subject matter are unique, only a locally prepared test can reflect the content and emphasis and constitute a suitable appraisal device. If the purpose is to measure certain broad outcomes common to many institutions, a published test may be quite suitable and, all factors considered, certainly less costly.

The timing of measurement constitutes another matter for decision. If students are expected to attain the objectives of the general education program during the first two years of college, measurement may logically be made at the end of that period. Often, evaluation at the end of the senior year also will be valuable in determining whether the outcomes in general education have been retained or in determining the effect of upper-class instruction on further attainment in this area.

Any tests used to measure outcomes in fields of major concentration will be more specific than those used to appraise general education outcomes. Nevertheless, they still should be focused on those aspects of specialization which are regarded as having permanent value. Here, again, a decision must be made whether to use locally prepared tests or published tests. While published tests seldom incorporate all the subject-matter and other instructional objectives of any single college department and may incorporate content that is not taught, they do contain much that is common to many programs. Some colleges, then, may well sacrifice the measurement of some of the outcomes they consider important in order to obtain data which can be utilized for certain types of comparisons, as, for example, in respect to those who will enter certain graduate schools, the comparison of the achievement of their own majors in chemistry with that of students trained elsewhere.

GROWTH STUDIES VERSUS STUDIES OF STATUS

It has already been suggested that at certain points in the students' careers information is needed concerning their development in reference to specified educational objectives. This information may be useful in several different ways. Primarily, it will show the extent to which instructional objectives are achieved after a specific amount of study. However, such measurements will not demonstrate how far students have progressed toward basic goals since first entering college. This question can be answered only if measurements of student performance are made prior to instruction and at appropriate intervals thereafter: at least two, and sometimes several, measurements will be needed if the college is to assess the development associated with its program: one, as students enter college; one, midway in their careers; one, near the terminal point of their formal education; and one, sometime after graduation to appraise continued intellectual development.

In setting up a plan for appraising growth, certain precautions must be observed. The first problem is that of defining purposes and selecting appropriate instruments. Second, an appraisal of outcomes of general education should focus on the knowledge, skills, and understanding which are the outcomes of required general education courses, or outcomes which can reasonably be expected from a college education, regardless of the specific courses or sequence of courses taken. Excluded are special outcomes, however desirable they may be, which may logically be associated only with certain kinds of studies not required of all students. Third, the instruments constructed or selected must produce dependable and pertinent information on the attainment of these outcomes. Fourth, to obtain comparable data, identical tests or their alternate forms should be used at each point in the process.

In addition to these general precautions, there are several more which are specific to the design of longitudinal studies. The study should include only those cases for whom complete measurement data are available since students who withdraw are likely to be less able than those who stay, and, unless they are eliminated from the group study, spurious gains will appear. For this reason, scores for freshmen who do not complete the sophomore year should be eliminated from the freshman data before freshman average scores are computed. Eliminating those for whom two sets of measurements are *not* available guarantees that the comparison is of the same students. Similar precaution should be observed for any later testings.

The analysis of results in the longitudinal study will require at the very minimum the computation of averages on each measure used for the freshman, sophomore, and senior groups and of the spread of the scores on each of the tests used. In addition it should be established that any differences that occur between these averages are not merely chance differences attributable to the unreliability of the measure used or to the smallness of the group or its lack of representativeness. Therefore, it is highly desirable that a statistic known as the "significance of the difference" be computed for each difference being studied.[2]

_____

[2] Statistics texts should be consulted both regarding the computation of this statistic and its interpretation, since there are a number of assumptions involved. For example, see chap. iii, "Small Sample Error Theory," in E. F. Lindquist, *Statistical Analysis in Educational Research* (Boston: Houghton Mifflin Co., 1940).

It should be borne in mind that often the error is made of establishing differences and the lack of differences too glibly on the basis of this statistic alone. It is a final step, to be taken only after the investigator is certain that other conditions of the research design have been fulfilled: all aspects of the change should have been considered, the measures used in evaluating the change should have been appropriate for each aspect, and such other factors as bias in the sampling, equivalence of learning opportunity, testing conditions, and the like should have been controlled. Sometimes a difference which is described as "significant" in the statistical sense is so merely because some one factor has not been controlled; the explanation for the difference, then, does not lie in any intrinsic aspect of the instructional program but in some peripheral condition and should not then be presented as a difference which is significant in an educational sense.

Assuming, however, that mean score differences are obtained that cannot be accounted for by chance or by extraneous bias, is this educationally significant? Not necessarily. Judgments of the educational importance of such improvements can be made only by the faculties concerned after a careful weighing of the test results against their teaching objectives. In some instances, small mean gains from one year to the next may be quite defensible. If, for example, small mean gains occur in areas where there is an interest only in a minimum level of proficiency, there may be no cause for concern. Similarly, if entering freshmen perform at a substandard level of achievement in some one area, there is no need to be unduly disturbed if achievement in that area in the sophomore year seems less than that in other areas where the students were more advanced initially.

There are instances when a college should be disturbed if students do not demonstrate a relatively large gain in the first two years; for example, in some area where it has designed and required a particular sequence of courses meant to develop specified skills or understanding. If students initially earn scores which are reasonable for entering freshmen but two years later earn scores below expectation, some explanation certainly should be sought, and there should be an examination of the adequacy of materials, methods, and other factors affecting student progress.

Thus far, the position has been taken that information on student development can best be obtained by first establishing a reference point at the freshman level and then obtaining second and/or third measurements at intervals thereafter. This is the ideal approach, but it has the disadvantage of requiring time for results to materialize. But often delay is impractical, say, when reorganization of a sequence of courses is being considered and immediate information on present outcomes is required before changes are initiated.

If this is the case, another approach may be useful, although it does have shortcomings in regard to measurement. This second approach assumes that the general caliber of students and their educational experiences in a given college and in a given span of time will not vary significantly—in other words, this year's sophomores are similar to what the present freshman students will be after they have completed two years, and, similarly, the present sophomores two years hence will be comparable to the current senior class. On this assumption, suitable measures are administered within the span of the same year to entering freshmen, end-of-year sophomores, and end-of-year seniors, and thus comparable data are obtained for study. This is known as the "horizontal" approach.

In general, data from a horizontal study should be treated in much the same way as in the longitudinal study, and mean scores should be computed and the statistical significance of mean differences tested. The analysis is the same as for the long-term study, with this major difference: in addition to reviewing all the usual factors which might account for differences, consideration must be given to the possibility of bias due to attrition and to the possibility that some degree of the difference may be attributable to unequal initial achievement levels of each class. In part, these risks can be minimized by matching the compared groups according to scores on scholastic aptitude and achievement tests which they took as freshmen. This precaution will not, however, control other factors that might affect one class but not another, such as changes in administration, faculty, and course requirements. When an important change of this kind has taken place, one of the basic assumptions for a horizontal study cannot be met. It is then ill-advised to use the horizontal approach since limitations of the data and subsequent difficulties of interpretation may prove insurmountable.

There are a number of situations in which a college may find it practical to take a dual approach to evaluating student development. If there is an immediate need for certain kinds of evidence, the college may begin by collecting data on a horizontal basis: all the currently enrolled students at academic levels of concern are tested within the same academic year, the data studied, and conclusions drawn. Thereafter provision is made to collect data on a longitudinal basis, with the freshmen being retested at the end of the sophomore year and again at the end of their senior year.

The obvious advantage to this compromise approach is that the college obtains data immediately from which to make tentative hypotheses about student development and, yet, testing the same individuals as they progress through the program assures more dependable data for later assessment of growth.

YEAR-TO-YEAR EVALUATION OF CLASSES AT THE SAME ACADEMIC LEVEL

The two types of studies just discussed are primarily intended to show how much students develop in relation to certain objectives as a result of the program of studies. There are, however, other ways of looking at the test data collected from such studies— or for that matter from any other measurement program which the college conducts—which are useful in providing other kinds of information frequently needed in college self-study. Among these is the year-to-year review of data collected on students at particular academic levels. Thus, in addition to following any given freshman class through college, it may also be advisable to learn how a particular freshman class compares with previous freshman classes. Is it, on the whole, as able? Is there a greater range of ability or a greater homogeneity of general ability or of preparation in certain basic subjects? When these students become sophomores or seniors, how do they compare with previous groups of sophomores and seniors? If this group started out at approximately the same achievement level as previous freshman groups, does it later reach comparable levels of performance? If differences are noted, what factors might account for them?

Comparisons of this kind help a college assess the effect of any specific change in its program. For example, when the humanities requirements are reorganized to provide for greater integration of its separate disciplines, are additional outcomes achieved? If other objectives are lost, is such loss justified in view of the new outcomes? Similarly, does the introduction of a new general education requirement in science create greater proficiency in an area of learning in which previous classes have been weak? Is this because the test does not measure the outcomes for which the college strives or does the course need further review and reorganization? Similar questions can be raised concerning other changes the college has made in recent years.

Comparisons of student achievement from one year to the next can be useful, even if innovations in the program have not been made recently. For instance, for one reason or another, a college may be largely perpetuating the basic elements of its program. Experimentation, if any, may be left to the initiative of individual instructors. Over a period of years the college has, perhaps, been generally satisfied with the types of students it attracts and with their over-all level of performance. There have been only minor variations among classes from year to year. Suddenly a change occurs in one direction or another. There may be a drop in student performance on the sophomore measures although there is every indication that the class is of the general caliber of previous classes. Errors in administering and scoring the tests or in computing average scores are always possible and, consequently, these operations should be re-examined. But, apart from errors, what factors might account for the change? Has there been a general easing-up of academic standards? Have students become more involved in certain kinds of extracurricular activities than in the past? Or has there been a somewhat unconscious change in emphasis in the instructional objectives so that the tests used no longer reflect the content and goals of certain basic courses? In the latter case, again it must be asked, are these changes for the better or worse; that is, should the changes in the instructional program be maintained and new tests built or selected, or should the tests be kept and the instructional program brought more in line with what the college considers to be its educational objectives?

Again, a college may find that, although the general caliber of incoming students is gradually improving, student accomplishments at the end of the sophomore or senior year maintain the same level as those of previous classes. Since it is reasonable to expect that the newer and more able students should perform at a higher level, there would be cause to consider why they are not doing so. Are the measures in use of sufficiently high "ceiling" to reflect a higher level of achievement? Are the students already so well prepared in certain areas that they are content to coast along on their previous background? Are there shortcomings in the instructional program in stimulating these more able groups of students; if so, can these be identified in any way?

Certain factors must be controlled before the answers to these questions can be obtained. Among these, the most important is to ascertain that the same tests or their alternate forms have been used. If in the interim there has been any change in the test used, comparisons cannot be drawn unless provision is made to equate the scores of the two tests. If this is not done, it cannot be said, for example, that a score equal to the published mean on Test X represents the same achievement as a score equal to the published mean on Test Y, for the subject matter of the tests, the difficulty levels of the questions, and the quality of the students used in standardization may all be different. Unless tables of equivalent scores have been developed, a college that has changed one or more tests in its program must accept the fact that the old and new data are not comparable and that, until there has been an opportunity to collect data on the new instruments, the kinds of comparisons discussed above are not justified.

Over and above the consideration of comparable data is the need to determine the statistical and educational significance of score differences observed from year to year. Just as with the longitudinal study, it is necessary to determine both whether the differences are greater than any that might be attributed to chance alone and how large a difference, either positive or negative, is educationally significant. While a simple statistical manipulation can determine the first type of significance, there are no formulae for determining educational significance; the importance of obtained differences can be assessed only when reviewed in terms of all of the local educational factors.

COMPARATIVE STUDIES AMONG DEPARTMENTS

The kinds of comparative studies suggested thus far have been related to determining the effectiveness of such general institutional provisions as might stem from particular admissions criteria, modifications in program requirements, faculty up-grading, new facilities, and the like. The total educational program is, however, made up of parts, and the effectiveness of these individual components must also be studied. For example, it may be advisable to appraise the caliber of departmental instruction. While such studies are obviously hazardous because of emotional overtones, and undoubtedly there are some members of the college community who believe that they should not be undertaken at all, nevertheless, they are part of any evaluation of the total institution. In such instances, it is much better to have a factual basis for comparisons than to rely on the subjective judgments either of the administrative staff or of the various departmental faculties.

One approach to departmental comparisons is through re-use of results from a college-wide testing program that was primarily intended to evaluate achievement in general education. The students might be classified by department or by field of study and the test results of each group studied to obtain leads concerning areas in which instruction appears to be strong or weak. If obtained differences for these student groups have statistical significance and seem to be large enough to have educational importance also, certain other factors should be weighed before the conclusion is drawn that poor instruction alone explains underachievement or, vice versa, that some one department is doing an unusually fine job. Perhaps students of one department are required to take but a single course in the area while in other areas a sequence of several courses is required. Possibly, facilities vary greatly by departments, or the faculty-student ratios differ. The quality of groups attracted to the area in the first place is a most important factor. And conceivably the portion of the test used to measure outcomes in a certain area may be less appropriate to the institution's objectives in that area than is true of the other fields measured by the test. These and other questions must be answered before final judgments are made but concomitantly the very process of raising and answering the questions is beneficial to all concerned and frequently will promote interdepartmental tolerance and understanding.

Comparisons of performance in major fields of concentration also are difficult to make. An obvious reason is that tests designed to measure the specialized outcomes of different fields are not directly comparable. How can the performance of a history major on a history test be compared with that of a physics major on a physics test? Each has a different background, and the tests have different content. It is like trying to decide whether one person is a better lawyer than another is a doctor. Since no absolute answer is available, it can be said only that among lawyers this person stands high and among surgeons the other person is not among the top-rankers—a comparison of sorts but not one which justifies an unequivocal conclusion.

Standardization data offer another means of evaluating departmental achievement. If the tests used in the various departments have all been standardized simultaneously on the basis of results obtained through their administration to students in the same groups of colleges, this standardization group can be used as a reference point. Thus, if the average score of history majors in College A on the history test is higher than the score achieved by 60 percent of the history majors in the standardization group, while the average score of the physics majors on the physics test is higher than the score made by only 20 percent of the physics majors in the standardization group, it can be said, and should be useful to know, that the relative standing of College A's history majors is higher than the relative standing of its physics majors. However, before concluding that this is the result of better instruction in history than in physics, some of the same kinds of questions raised above in regard to quality of group, facilities, student-teacher ratio, and the suitability of the tests should be raised. The first and most obvious point to consider is whether the history test more closely reflects the content and emphasis of the major program in history than the physics test does in relation to the program in physics. Presumably, the question about the test should have been raised before it was administered, but it is possible that the physics test actually is less suitable than it was originally judged to be.

USE OF NORMS IN COLLEGE COMPARISONS

The increase in student achievement on general education outcomes from the freshman to senior year, or the trend in achievement over a period of years, can be determined from local data alone without recourse to normative data. Thus, a college certainly need not use published tests for studies of this type if it believes that locally prepared tests more closely represent its curriculum. However, it may be desired to evaluate the effectiveness of an institution's efforts through comparison of its students' achievement with that of students in other colleges.

In the abstract, such studies have considerable merit because they offer colleges the opportunity to compare themselves with an outside standard of success. Theoretically, this should prevent a college from becoming too inbred in its efforts—a possibility if performance is reviewed solely in terms of local standards. In practice, however, comparative studies are not quite so valuable, for at least two reasons. First, no absolute standard of success exists for all institutions, and, second, the very nature of the preparation of published tests presents measurement difficulties.

In building tests for wide distribution, every effort is made to design tests in terms of the kinds of objectives and materials typically included in the greatest number of college courses, but it must be recognized that the tests may not measure all the objectives that any individual college promotes nor reflect the same balance of offerings. It follows then that, although a test may represent a college program in a number of important ways, it rarely fits perfectly; if it includes a number of areas there will be complications of inequalities of appropriateness from subject to subject, with, say, the biology section corresponding well, the mathematics test less well, and so on. The extent to which the study can tolerate some inappropriateness and still produce useful results must be decided by each institution.

The second problem mentioned above relates to the norms

group upon which tests are standardized. Comparison with a larger norms group is necessary if a local college is to make nonprovincial judgments. But for these comparisons to be meaningful, the colleges represented in the groups should have similar objectives and offerings, should enroll students of substantially the same level of scholastic aptitude, and should have similar educational and financial resources.

Quite obviously these conditions are rarely met. The norms group is seldom so completely defined that it is easy to assess the extent to which it represents a reasonable base for comparison. Thus, once again, a college must be prepared to determine the degree of compromise it can make in this regard and still profit by the experience. Because the factors of test content and the composition of the norms group are never perfectly tenable, the data obtained from comparative studies of this type are always to a certain extent incomplete. Also, it is not always easy to work with data that have limitations of this type since additional local limitations can be obscured. For example, if a college fares well by comparison with the larger norms group, there may be a tendency to feel oversecure and let the matter rest, when actually the norms were an inappropriate base for comparison; or, if the comparison is less favorable, there is often a natural tendency to explain away the differences solely in terms of test content or of differences between the local group and the norms group and, once again, to let the matter rest. In either case, a serious effort should have been made to understand why the results turned out as they did. If the performance seems superior to that of the larger group, surely it could be worthwhile to look at the local picture to determine what aspects of the program seem to be particularly strong so that they may be perpetuated and even improved. Or, if the results are less favorable, it could be beneficial to review the present program and resources of the college in an attempt to identify reasons for this and then plan to strengthen the college in these respects.

Occasionally, there may be no particular need to modify practices if the local results appear in a somewhat unfavorable light with respect to the norms group. The local college may have some goals which are not universally held by the colleges represented in the norms group; all it may wish is to learn whether its students are reaching some desirable minimum level of proficiency in the goals measured by the tests. If this point is achieved, the college quite properly feels no compulsion to adopt the practices of any other college or group of colleges. Even in this situation, however, such comparisons may serve as a useful point of departure for a study of local objectives, policies, practices, and outcomes and will help to place them in some perspective.

STUDIES OF NONCOGNITIVE FACTORS

Most institutions are concerned about the development in their students of certain kinds of attitudes and appreciations, social and vocational skills, worthwhile personal interests, and the like. Therefore, if a college hopes to achieve a balance in its evaluation, it should gather evidence also on how well such goals as these are being achieved. There have been some very interesting explorations along these lines, which are well worth attention.

Some of the types of studies which have already been discussed are appropriate for measuring noncognitive outcomes. The major difference between them lies in the types of data-gathering devices they employ. Since most noncognitive outcomes fall in the realm of so-called intangibles, which are not adaptable to linear measurement, it is more difficult to locate or develop instruments which provide the same degree of dependability as do achievement measures.[3] That this is likely to be so should not, however, deter a college from undertaking an evaluation of noncognitive outcomes, for if the outcomes are defined as concretely as possible and the study suitably designed and executed, despite limitations, there will be results more indicative than uninformed hunches or opinions. But always it must be recognized that the data do have limitations.

Some of the studies of a noncognitive nature may emerge from the materials of regular testing programs. For example, if freshman testing includes measures of personal qualities, it may be of value to ascertain from them what proportion of the students appear to have relatively serious adjustment problems. Similar information can also be obtained from admission applications and

[3] For a general discussion of the types of instruments available for measuring noncognitive factors, with a discussion of their major limitations, see chap. 5 of the present book.

biographic questionnaires submitted by entering students. The information thus gained may influence decisions regarding the kind of guidance services to be provided. Consideration of additional data from other incoming classes, along with the review of data from the guidance bureau, can be used in determining whether or not the services should be expanded or changed. Or, again, attitudes toward certain beliefs, groups, or institutions can be assessed at the time of entrance and reappraised several years later to see whether efforts to inculcate certain basic points of view have been successful.

These and other similar sources of information provide general background data on the needs and strengths of students which can never be obtained from scholastic records and tests alone. Used in conjunction with the latter, data on noncognitive factors help to round out the picture of a group of students, sharpening the grey areas and bringing particular features into focus. And over a period of time, they present descriptions of student characteristics which both the instructional faculty and the administrative staff can use to improve student services, curricular and extracurricular activities, and the like.

The reader who is interested in pursuing considerations in testing in noncognitive areas will want to examine several published studies. The final report of the Cooperative Study of Evaluation in General Education of the American Council on Education contains a discussion of the approaches used by a faculty group working together under the direction of Paul L. Dressel to produce instruments that would help in assessing development in those values stressed in general education.[4] Two of the several reports of the earlier Cooperative Study in General Education, conducted under the direction of Ralph W. Tyler, describe some of the instruments that were developed in that project.[5] One of the most

[4] Dressel and Mayhew, chap. viii, "Pervasive Objectives: Attitudes," *op. cit.*

[5] Paul J. Brouwer, "Identifying and Meeting Common Needs," *Student Personnel Services in General Education* (Washington: American Council on Education, 1949), pp. 57 ff.

Harold B. Dunkel, *General Education in the Humanities* (Washington: American Council on Education, 1947). A goals of life inventory, a religious concepts inventory, and an inventory of the arts are reproduced in the Appendix and discussed in the text.

recently published works in this area is a study by Philip E. Jacob of the impact of their education on the values held by college students at the time of their entrance to college.[6] Also, there are bibliographies of personality inventories. One source for locating these is the issues of the *Review of Educational Research* on growth, development, and learning.[7]

ALUMNI SURVEYS

All the foregoing approaches to institutional evaluation share one major limitation: they provide information on student development only for a narrowly defined period of time—the two- or four-year academic sequence. In the final analysis, what its graduates are like may be much more indicative of an institution's success in accomplishing its major purposes. Thus, efforts to evaluate effectiveness are not complete until a serious attempt has been made to obtain further information from alumni about those outcomes which the college considers to be of special importance.

What is pertinent information will vary from one institution to another, but all will be concerned with obtaining information on how former students appear to fulfill major goals in intellectual, vocational, social, and personal areas. For example, if a college emphasized preprofessional training, it should learn what proportion of alumni complete advanced training. Similarly, it should know how many are placed in their chosen fields and what positions they hold. Information on the scope and depth of current reading habits and other activities, both recreational and civic, also indicate to a degree success in developing worthwhile understandings and appreciations. And graduates' opinions, in retrospect, about the education which they received, or certain features of it, are worthy of consideration.

Most alumni surveys have been based on data gathered through interviews, questionnaires, or both. Tests would also be useful in measuring the extent to which certain intellectual outcomes have

---

[6] Philip E. Jacob, *Changing Values in College* (New York: Harper & Bros., 1057). A digest appears in the *NEA Journal*, January 1958.

[7] American Educational Research Association, "Growth, Development and Learning," *Review of Educational Research*, 15: 473 ff., December 1955 (most recent issue).

been retained or improved, but obviously there are practical problems involved in asking alumni to take tests.

The questionnaire can be subject to considerable misunderstanding when questions are not clearly phrased. The interview circumvents this difficulty to a large extent since the interviewers can make certain that the interviewees do understand. For this reason and because a greater proportion of the alumni approached are likely to cooperate, interviews give greater assurance of usable responses than do questionnaires. But the interview is usually a much more costly procedure. Questionnaires are therefore more generally used, and so it may be pertinent to discuss here some of the ways in which their disadvantages can be lessened.

First, alumni should be told the basic purposes of the questionnaire. A clear, brief, and inviting statement aimed at rousing their interest and cooperation should suffice. Also, they should be assured that their reply will be treated in a confidential manner. Without sacrificing the major purposes of the study, the questionnaire should be kept as brief and uncomplicated as possible. Questions should be so stated that everyone will understand their intent. To guarantee this, it is well to try out the questions in advance with a small group.

A decision must be made about the number of alumni to be included in the study. For small or relatively new colleges the study may well include all alumni. For colleges with large alumni bodies a representative sample will do. In either case, returns must be large enough to assure a dependable interpretation.[8] If the responses of the alumni in general are to be studied, a smaller number of questionnaires will suffice. If, however, the design of the study requires an analysis of responses by certain subcategories, such as alumni of five years' standing versus those of ten years', or by major programs, and so forth, a larger number will be needed.[9]

Attention must be given to the details of due dates and follow-ups. When there is little personal involvement, returns from ques-

[8] For bibliography on sampling, see Francis G. Cornell, "Sample Surveys in Education," *Review of Educational Research,* 14:359, December 1954.

[9] For considerations in sampling, see Helen M. Walker and Joseph Lev, *Statistical Inference* (New York: Henry Holt & Co., 1953), which includes a section on sampling and survey design.

tionnaires are discouragingly slow and small. Responses will increase with the amount and kind of additional follow-up. Some alumni surveys have produced returns varying from 50 to 74 percent.

In analyzing data from questionnaires, consideration must be given to the possibilities of bias in the replies. Did proportionately more men than women reply? More local alumni than alumni at a distance? More younger than older alumni? More who graduated in the upper half of their classes than in the lower half? And so forth. When such questions are not satisfactorily answered, interpretations should be qualified accordingly.

Analysis with no attempt to relate to factors known about the alumni as students can be quite useful in obtaining evidence on how well certain long-range objectives have been attained. But analysis can be strengthened if responses are categorized by patterns of characteristics or experiences that the alumni shared as students and provide an opportunity to relate their present status to past educational experiences. Analysis may reveal experiences which seem to correlate with the attainment of certain objectives, or the converse, and help thereby to support judgments concerning the adequacy of certain basic policies and practices.

The reader planning an alumni questionnaire will certainly find it helpful to examine several alumni questionnaire studies. Some questionnaires that have been published or could be obtained are those of: the Univeristy of Syracuse,[10] the University of Minnesota,[11] the Woman's College of the University of North Carolina,[12] and Chatham College.[13]

EVALUATION, A CONTINUING PROCESS

From time to time changes occur in the student body, the faculty, the curricular offerings, the leadership, and the general

[10] C. Robert Pace, "Follow-up Studies of College Graduation," in *Growing Points in Educational Research* (Washington: American Educational Research Assoc., 1949).
[11] C. Robert Pace, *They Went to College* (Minneapolis: University of Minnesota, 1941).
[12] Woman's College of the University of North Carolina, *The Alumnae News* (Greensboro, N.C.), April 1956, pp. 12 ff.
[13] Office of Evaluation Services, *Bulletins;* available from Chatham College, Pittsburgh 32, Pa.

academic atmosphere of an institution. Whether these changes are the result of systematic planning or circumstance, the institution should be aware of them and prepared to measure their effects. But it is difficult, if not impossible, to do this when no information exists on the status of students before and after the occurrence of the change. Infrequent and sporadic efforts at evaluation do not produce the required continuity. Therefore, to be effective in facilitating institutional study, evaluation must be continuous and according to plan.

7. Administering the Testing Program

THE EXTENT AND COMPLEXITY OF ADMINISTRATIVE ARRANGEMENTS for test programs depend on a number of factors, the first of which is the educational philosophy of the institution—how it views its responsibilities to students and how many special services dependent on testing it believes it should provide.

The institution that offers only a program of freshman tests in order to gain general background data on the group may manage quite well administratively with limited advisory services and the part-time attention of a faculty or administrative staff member. This arrangement is typical in institutions that initiate modest test programs, usually with the intention of gradual expansion. In contrast, institutions having highly developed evaluation programs and large universities that are naturally complex in organization will utilize a very large staff of administrators and specialists to engage in a wide variety of evaluation activities.

Currently a number of kinds of administrative organization for evaluation programs are in use. A few institutions centralize administration in the hands of a specially trained evaluation officer who receives his authority from a dean or the president. He probably uses a faculty advisory committee in connection with each phase of his activities or, perhaps, a single general advisory committee in over-all planning. This kind of plan provides the best opportunity for general coordination. At some institutions, a member of the education or psychology department carries a similar responsibility. At still others the responsibility may lie with a faculty committee whose chairman assumes direction, usually with a concurrent reduction in his teaching load. A complex setup is found where there are boards of specialists, with one over-all officer (who may be one of the administrative officers of the institution or an expert trained in some phase of evaluation), teachers who assist test specialists in building achievement tests, a person who specializes in vocational testing and advising, a psychometrist

97

who administers supplementary tests to individuals, a statistician, and other miscellaneous staff. Sometimes the personnel of each board represent chiefly the interests of a particular unit of the institution, such as a school of engineering or an office of admissions.

Organization for evaluation, then, can be completely centralized with one board or person responsible for test activities; completely decentralized with each unit—school, department, and so forth— operating independently in designing and conducting its own program; or decentralized, with certain services being handled by one officer and latitude given to individual units to develop supplementary programs.

ORGANIZATION AND FUNCTIONS

Whether the organization is complex or simple, the procedures should reflect the educational philosophy of the institution. To guarantee this and also to ensure that its operation keeps abreast of student and institutional needs, the evaluation unit—however it is constituted—should have the guidance of an advisory committee made up of administrative and faculty personnel to help formulate and clarify policies and work plans, suggest areas needing examination, promote cooperation with other units of administration and faculty, and act generally as a sounding board. The directing person should know to whom he is responsible, have ready access to faculty or staff in handling particular problems, and have a budget.

Because certain functions of the program are of a recurring nature, procedures can be established for handling them both efficiently and expeditiously. Thus the staff is free to turn to new projects and services, for in any active institution an evaluation project by its nature suggests areas needing exploration. Here, again the advice of a steering committee is needed to establish priorities so that the main objectives of the program will not be lost in the pursuit of less important, albeit interesting, data.

Regular functions

The nature of the test activities described in previous chapters indicates the regular functions of the person who carries responsibility for testing in a comprehensive program: (1) supervising testing programs for purposes of admissions, guidance, and institutional evaluation; (2) assisting the faculty to improve their measures of the results of instruction; (3) supervising testing programs that support particular educational policies or curriculum analysis, such as progression on the basis of achievement, admission to an upper division, selection for a graduate program, establishment of courses based on student needs; (4) informing faculty and students of outside testing programs such as the National Teacher Examinations; the National Science Foundation test programs; the Graduate Record Area Tests; miscellaneous city, state, and federal civil service tests; and premedical, prelaw, and other preprofessional tests; (5) selecting tests for special groups, say, for evaluating the progress of a group of students receiving remedial work in speech, or for individual students who can be given better guidance if specialized test data are available; (6) planning the analysis of test data needed for meaningful interpretations for all test activities; and (7) providing guidance and technical assistance in the construction of testing instruments for experimental use in instruction. Clearly, the guiding officer must be competent in administrative matters and either be professionally trained in evaluation or have advisory or staff resources to meet these needs.

Special functions

In some institutions, the administrative officer or committee also supervises, for example, the reproduction of test copy, the arrangements for final examinations and make-up examinations, the scoring of examination papers, arrangements for administration of noninstitutional tests as a form of cooperation in national standardization programs, and perhaps the administration of tests or scoring services for neighbor institutions. He, or they, may also be responsible for institutional studies that do not involve tests or test data, such as the collection of enrollment data for an analysis of student mortality—but it is not within the province of this guide to pursue these aspects of the job.

While the best arrangement is that which coordinates most of these activities into one unit, some of them can be shared by other college or university officers, so that special service may be provided even without a special staff. In fact, this is probably the rule rather than the exception in the organization of evaluation activities.

PROBLEMS OF TEST SELECTION

The question of who should select published (as opposed to locally constructed) tests depends in large measure on the types of tests to be included in the program. For example, interest inventories and personality tests will generally be selected by someone who has had considerable training and experience in testing and guidance. However, it is the faculty who should appraise achievement tests in each subject area being measured to determine relevancy to content and objectives of the curriculum, although the advice of a measurement specialist on the technical characteristics of the test should be sought.

Validity

A glance at the test title, the catalogue description, and even the description of the test provided in a test manual, is *not* a sufficient basis for judging whether a test will be appropriate for the purpose the college has in mind. The test itself must be closely examined and such evidence as is available on it evaluated. Thus, if the purpose is to obtain information from a test on a student's chances of doing successful work in languages, the relationship between scores attained on the test and academic performance in languages should be known. The college should ascertain in advance what kinds of abilities the test measures, and it should evaluate the subparts and items of the test to determine whether, on a logical basis, they fit the defined purposes of the test.

However, since what appears logical on an a priori basis may not always work in practice, the college should know whether the test has been used with students similar to its own and with what success. Test manuals frequently contain information on this type of test validity.[1] Also current psychological and educational literature on testing are sources of information, as are critical reviews

[1] See Edward E. Cureton, "Validity," in E. F. Lindquist (ed.), *Educational Measurement*, p. 621. This is a most complete discussion of the question of test validity and one which is most helpful to anyone who is seriously interested in pursuing the subject: statistical problems, formulae, assumptions, and the like are considered.

of the tests found in mental measurements textbooks and in the *Mental Measurements Yearbooks*.[2]

Usually, the predictive validity of tests is obtained by determining the degree of correspondence between test scores and whatever one is trying to predict, frequently grade-point averages. The relationship found is most frequently summarized by a numerical index called the coefficient of validity.[3] A validity coefficient for a test is by no means a fixed statistic. It may vary with different classes and even with the way a course is taught in different years. An instructor who uses an objective test as a measure of achievement of English composition skills may find the validity coefficient varying from year to year with growth of his own instructional effectiveness. However, it is reasonable to suppose that if he once developed a test with an acceptable validity coefficient for stable course objectives, that coefficient would not shift greatly in subsequent administrations to the same kinds of students. On the other hand, on a given test the coefficient used to identify students who need remedial reading and that used to identify students with high reading literacy could be quite different. For this reason the worth of a test as expressed by one or more validity coefficients must be considered in terms of the purposes the test will serve.

Apart from the fact that a particular test might not be a valid predictor of success, validity coefficients may vary in size for several other reasons: the consistency with which the test measures the area in question, the size of the group studied, the range of ability within the group, the standard used to determine success, and so on. Since interpretation of coefficients is no task for the novice, advice of a trained technician must be sought for their meaning. Suffice it to say here that in selecting achievement tests, correspondence between course objectives and test content is the primary consideration, and should be determined by the instructional staff.

Reliability

A test, to be effective, should yield consistent results, so that the user can place confidence in the score a student obtains. That is to say, if this student were to take this test or a comparable form

---

[2] Oscar K. Buros (ed.), *Mental Measurements Yearbooks* (Highland Park, N.J.: Gryphon Press). The last edition is the fourth, published in 1953.
[3] Cureton in *Educational Measurement*, pp. 680 ff.

of it again, he would obtain a similar score or a similar rank order within the tested group.

In general, tests (and their subparts) can reach a high standard of consistency if they are sufficiently long, cover a homogeneous body of material, are free from technical inadequacies such as ambiguity, and can be scored precisely. However, because there are always uncontrolled factors in any test administration, no test will ever yield perfectly consistent or reliable results.

The consistency, or dependability, of a test is an especially important criterion in selecting tests to be used to evaluate the strengths and weaknesses of an individual student for diagnostic and guidance purposes. If the objective is to obtain a general picture of how a group of students compares with similar groups of students, the test need not always meet the highest standards of test consistency, although it is desirable that it do so.

Information on the dependability of test scores is usually provided in test manuals in one or more of several different ways. A most useful kind of report is that which provides information on the probability that if a student is retested, his score will fall not more than a certain number of score points above or below his hypothetical average (true) score. This is a statistic known as the "probable error of measurement."

Since no test is perfectly reliable, each time a student is tested, he earns a slightly different score. Thus, if we were to give an infinite number of comparable forms of a test to an individual, his scores would vary between certain extremes, with the majority of the scores clustering around a given point, which would be the average score for that individual on that test. This theoretical average score is called his true score. The probable error of measurement then is the range in score points above or below this hypothetical average score, which includes 50 percent of the obtained scores. If the probable error of measurement on a test is 2.5 and if a student earns a score of 52, there is a fifty-fifty chance that if he were tested many times his average, or true, score would lie somewhere between 49.5 and 54.5. The more dependable the test, the smaller the range of scores.[4]

[4] Naturally the difference must be related to the difficulty of the test and to its range of scores; a difference of 75 in a test with a range of 500 points is not large; a difference of 75 in a test with a range of 125 is large.

The degree to which a test yields consistent results is also indicated by its coefficient of reliability. There are several ways of computing this coefficient.[5] Basically, it is a mathematical description of the relationship between two sets of scores on the same test or alternate forms of the test when they are administered under identical circumstances. The closer this relationship, the higher is the reliability coefficient and the smaller are the chances that a given student's relative position within a group will shift from one testing to another. As the reliability coefficient decreases, less and less reliance can be placed on a score as a measure of a student's performance in respect to the abilities measured by the test.

A general working rule is that if a test is to be used with an individual student, the coefficient should not fall below .90, although it is best that it be .95 or higher. For group comparisons and group prediction the coefficient of reliability should never be lower than .60. Ordinarily, however, it should be at least .80, and it is desirable that it be even higher.

As with coefficients of validity, coefficients of reliability are not simple to interpret, since much depends upon understanding the assumptions involved in any of the several ways in which they may be computed and on the uses to which the test scores are to be put. At this phase of test selection it is usually best to seek the advice of a person with wide experience in testing.

Difficulty

In addition to the selection factors already discussed, tests should be evaluated in terms of their level of difficulty. If a test is either too easy or too difficult, the scores will not discriminate adequately among students. (Discrimination is usually the objective, although there are some exceptions.) For most testing purposes, scores for a given group should range from the low to the high end of the scale with about half the scores clustering around the middle.

The difficulty of a test is determined by an analysis of the test questions in terms of the types of materials teachers believe that students are able to handle. Evidence of how the test has functioned for other groups is also helpful. In any event, just as with the

[5] See Robert L. Thorndike, "Reliability," in *Educational Measurement,* p. 560.

validity of the test, one should not rely wholly upon the statements made in the test manual. This does not by any means imply that test authors are unscrupulous in their reporting. It simply means that truly representative groups exist chiefly in theory—what is easy for one group may be quite difficult for another.

Adequacy of norms

The *raw score* of a test is simply the number of correct responses, although it may also be the number of correct responses reduced[6] by the number of wrong responses or some fraction thereof. Although parts of scores are sometimes weighted, if the items are homogeneous and sampling of the field has been comprehensive, weighting adds little, if anything, to the result.[7] From the raw scores and their statistical manipulation, the examiner can ascertain a student's relative position in his group, his deviation from the average of the group, the general difficulty of the test, its correlation with any previous or later tests used, and the like. Thus, in simplest terms, the classroom teacher who is accustomed to writing tests and has general knowledge of his students gains further information from raw scores by means of ranking, averaging, and determining deviations from the average.

When test results for larger and less intimately known groups (as for a whole class of sophomores) are to be studied or when the performance of students is to be considered in terms that are not related to their immediate environment (as for a class in qualitative analysis with students in other colleges taking this course), the test user turns to norms. Sometimes before published norms can be used, the raw scores must be converted into whatever "unit of measure" is employed by the test publisher.[8]

Norms are most commonly reported in terms of percentile rank, a means of relating gross rankings of scores to the proportion of students in one hundred earning scores below a given point. Ac-

[6] For a discussion of the problem of correction for guessing, see Traxler in *Educational Measurement*, pp. 347–51.

[7] For a discussion of the considerations in weighting, see Traxler in *Educational Measurement*, pp. 369–71.

[8] See John C. Flanagan, "Units, Scores, and Norms," in *Educational Measurement*, pp. 695 ff.; or see E. F. Lindquist, *A First Course in Statistics* (New York: Houghton Mifflin Co., 1942), pp. 145 ff.

cording to this practice, a student with a percentile rank of 34 has a score that has been exceeded by 66 percent of the students in the normative group.

Raw scores may also be converted into "standard score units" to establish their positions above and below the average (or mean) score. This is done, initially, by giving the test to a large group of students (normative group) and computing the average score, as well as the "standard deviation," which summarizes the way in which the scores distribute above and below the mean. By appropriate equations the raw scores can be converted into a convenient standard scale. All later raw scores are also corrected to the same scale and have meaning in terms of the performance of the original group tested. These scores are called standard scores or *scaled scores.*[9]

But, again, the user of this or any other scale needs to be aware of the characteristics of the normative group. For example, if a college serves students who are from families educationally underprivileged, say from an impoverished town and uses results from a published general aptitude test of good reputation as a basis for admission, it will probably not use the cutting points or the percentile norms provided in the test manual since the normative group is of a different caliber. Provided the examination content does not penalize the educationally underprivileged group in particular and *provided* the scale is divorced from other populations and new norms are established on the basis of the underprivileged group or other groups like them, it is proper to utilize the examination and its scale.[10]

Obviously, the original sample of students (the norms group) upon whose test performance the scales are computed becomes all-important. If this group is biased in any way, comparing the performance of the local group with the normative group is inappropriate. Furthermore, in utilizing the norms, the user must ascertain that the norms population is one with which it is reasonable to compare one's own students. Local data will help the college

[9] To study the problem of scaling tests, see Flanagan in *Educational Measurement,* chap. 17.

[10] For a discussion of the inadequacies of some tests for underprivileged groups, see Allison Davis, *Social-Class Influences Upon Learning* (Cambridge, Mass.: Harvard University Press, 1948).

evaluate how well a student compares with students who have had identical instructional opportunity in its own institution or, in the case of an entering group, with students of the caliber selected for, or patronizing—as the case may be—the college. Thus, the lack of relevant norms need not prevent a college from using a test which is otherwise well suited to its purposes.[11]

Comparable forms

Tests that are published in two or more comparable forms lend themselves to more uses than tests that have but one form, for students may be retested to measure progress, breaches of test security are less likely to occur, and, in special cases where scores obtained by students seem open to question, the results may be checked by administering another form.

When there is a need to select tests with comparable or equivalent forms, it is desirable to examine the tests to determine whether they are indeed comparable. (It should be borne in mind that no amount of statistical operation can make two tests embodying different objectives comparable; they must have basic common objectives and content before statistical equating of scores can be meaningful.) Questions to be reviewed are: Do both forms cover the same content and objectives? Have various types of materials received approximately the same emphasis? Do the test items seem to be of equal difficulty? Can results on both forms be interpreted similarly? In addition to examining the test itself, the opinions of experts who are familiar with the technical problems inherent in developing comparable forms are useful in obtaining answers to some of these questions as is, again, the evidence published in the manual and in the literature.

Completeness of manual

If the test is accompanied by adequate information concerning its development, validity, and reliability; if it has clear directions for administering and scoring; and if adequate descriptions of its

[11] A very clear discussion of some of the factors which operate to affect norms, and the difficulties of publishers in supplying generally suitable norms, will be found in *Test Service Bulletin*, No. 39 (New York: Psychological Corporation, May 1950); available upon request from the Corporation, 522 Fifth Ave., New York, N.Y.

norms are provided, one may say that a test has a complete manual. This material should be organized for easy use. Also it should contain information on skills and abilities that the tests and sub-tests measure, on the difficulty level of each item, and suggestions for the teacher, counselor, or administrator that will help each make the fullest use of the test results.

Miscellaneous points

Other points to consider in selecting a test are (*a*) cost, both of basic materials and of scoring and interpretation; (*b*) format of the test; (*c*) the probability of its future availability, if a long-range program is contemplated; and (*d*) the feasibility of administration of the test under whatever local conditions of staff and division of class periods obtain.

THE MECHANICS OF TESTING

In embarking upon a program of evaluation, the sponsoring group should consider problems of the mechanics of the operation. It will want to ascertain, in particular, that provisions are made in advance for administration, scoring, test reproduction, the analysis of the results, and reporting to faculty and students.

Administration, scoring, and reproduction

Needless to say, administration should both be planned carefully in advance and carried through in all its aspects with meticulous attention to detail. Inexperienced examiners will do well to review the manuals of some of our better tests that give explicit instructions on administration, many of which are universal in application. The long experience of the College Entrance Examination Board in conducting its examinations has resulted in an excellent manual entitled *Supervisor's Handbook;* it may be purchased from Educational Testing Service for a nominal sum.[12] Traxler discusses test administration in detail in *Educational Measurement.*[13] For inexperienced examiners these two items will be very helpful.

[12] Address: Educational Testing Service, Box 592, Princeton, N.J.
[13] Pp. 329 ff.

Accurate scoring of tests is also requisite to valid and usable test results. Whether the tests are hand- or machine-scored, there are good and bad practices relative to such matters as preparation of the most suitable scoring key, handling of keys, rechecking for accuracy, recording the results, and so on. Since these have been described by Traxler, they need not be recounted here.[14]

Test reproduction has also been fully treated elsewhere, by Spaulding,[15] who has described the various types of reproduction processes suitable for tests.

Statistical treatment of results

A testing program that has reached the analysis stage is nearing the point where it will begin to serve the purposes for which it was established. However, in order to bridge the final gap between meaningless numbers and useful descriptive information, the data must be subjected to further systematic treatment. Such questions as how an entering class compares with classes entering other institutions or with another year's entering class, what a particular student's academic strengths and weaknesses are, whether a revised natural science program has achieved expected objectives, and the like, can be considered only after the data are statistically analyzed and interpreted according to some defined reference standard, such as local or published norms.

Thus, in almost all instances there will be a need to determine the score which describes the average performance of the group tested. In addition to this statistic, whether it be the median or the mean, information on the range of ability represented in the group will also be needed. This may be done roughly by computing such specific measures of score variation as the interquartile range or the standard deviation. Which of these statistics is used depends on the kinds of analyses to be made later. Usually the median and interquartile range suffice, but if correlational analysis is planned, means and standard deviations will be needed.

A brief review of the uses of statistical information for various

[14] *Ibid.,* pp. 329–68.
[15] Geraldine Spaulding, "Reproducing the Test," in *Educational Measurement,* pp. 417 ff.

purposes will point up both the kinds of information that can be gained and their importance. This discussion will necessarily be sketchy since descriptions of statistical techniques fall outside the scope of the present work.

The *admissions* program uses several kinds of information—test scores, rank in class, and principal's rating. Since there is normally a need to compare the standings of candidates on the various criteria, more precise predictions of success can be obtained if the relationship between the selection criteria and grade-point averages is studied. Local norms, percentage of agreement among the criteria and between the criteria of selection and the eventual outcome in terms of student success (coefficients of correlation), and expectancy tables based on this agreement are essential, though these need not be computed annually when criteria are well established.

Guidance, like selection, involves prediction, and for immediate purposes the primary point of departure is the local competitive group. All the data needed for selection purposes are useful as well as data showing the relationship of ability and previous achievement in specific programs of study. The test results will eventually be used to help students understand their skills and abilities; thus, individual profile charts which plot strengths and weaknesses are helpful. For other guidance purposes, such as interest testing, comparisons with larger norms groups are advisable.

The use of tests in *course placement* is in many respects like that in admissions. It differs in that predictions are made within very narrowly defined areas—the probability of success within a specific course. Local data are all-important. Test scores should be related to success in the course, and experience or expectancy tables are helpful in establishing appropriate cutting points. In some cases, placement will not involve prediction as much as appraisal of current status: How does this student compare with students who have successfully completed a given course? Here scatter plots which compare test scores with grades or other qualitative descriptions of successful students in the course are relevant.

Instructional uses of tests, like the purposes thus far mentioned, require primarily reference to local data. How the class as a whole performs on the test and the range of proficiency represented are the points of major concern. Measures of central tendency and scatter will be needed. On occasion, comparisons with published norms will be useful, as may be annual comparisons between classes. Analysis of subscores within the test will show the extent to which teaching objectives in a course are being met. Item analyses will reveal the difficulty of particular categories of materials and also be useful in improving the test for future use. Sometimes comparisons of gains between pre- and post-tests will be required. At other times the need will be for special studies to evaluate the success of one teaching approach over another.

Institutional surveys for planning and curricular purposes make greater use of published norms since comparisons from one group to another will be needed. Usually, the statistical significance of the differences between groups must be ascertained, which necessitates computing the mean and standard deviation as a first step.[16] Graphic presentations of data in bar charts or histograms may prove helpful.

Although the above discussion is sketchy, the general methods for certain approaches have been suggested in the specific chapters dealing with the major testing purpose. A beginner should not attempt to put any of the methods into use until he has referred to some standard text in statistics.

Above all, whatever measurement is undertaken must be made meaningful to all concerned by keeping them informed about plans, by enlisting their assistance at strategic points, and by relating all work realistically to the educational process. This usually means group meetings with faculty and with students to clarify the purposes of testing programs that are of special concern to them. It means providing summaries of findings in a form that can be understood and utilized by those who need them. It undoubtedly means maintaining a level of contagious enthusiasm for the objectives of each project and not getting bogged down

[16] See E. F. Lindquist, *Statistical Analysis in Educational Research* (Boston: Houghton Mifflin Co., 1940), pp. 54 ff. Discusses methods of computing and interpreting significance of mean difference.

by what can often become a bewildering mass of data. It means also remaining sufficiently alert to the needs of officers, groups, and individuals within the institution to be in a position to relate available instruments or data to their current problems.

REPORTING TO STUDENTS AND FACULTY

When a report is made to a student, it is advisable to give him, not only his raw scores, but as much of the following information as possible: (1) He should have some point of reference, such as his local class or group or a preceding class or group, with which to compare his own scores; it may be possible to do this by using a simple distribution of scores and by marking his position in the distribution. (2) When it is relevant, he should be able, similarly, to compare his scores with those of students at other institutions. (3) In certain tests, it will be profitable for him to compare his scores with his own performance at a previous time or to compare his relative achievement on the various tests and their subparts; this is more complicated, requiring, as a minimum, percentile scores referred to some basic group or the use of some form of standard score.[17] Usually the purposes of the tests should be reiterated since students quickly forget such things.

A report to the instructional staff concerned with the test should begin with a review of the purposes for which the test was administered and indicate to what extent the purposes were realized; in addition it should tell them what they can expect to learn from the data as they are presented, what the salient facts are about local results and about the results obtained elsewhere, and how much statistical significance can be attached to the averages and to the individual scores in terms of the concept of variability in scores.[18] Sometimes graphic presentations are more readily grasped than tabular data; these are discussed in standard texts.[19]

[17] Flanagan in *Educational Measurement,* pp. 722 ff., discusses test scaling and various procedures for identifying the best scaling method for a particular situation; additional bibliography on standard scores is given at end of chapter.

[18] See any standard textbook for discussions of test score variability. The reader may consult, for instance, Henry E. Garrett, *Statistics in Education and Psychology* (4th ed.; New York: Longmans, Green & Co., 1953), chap. iii; or Lindquist, *A First Course in Statistics,* pp. 69 ff.; or Karl J. Holzinger, *Statistical Methods for Students in Education* (Boston: Ginn & Co., 1928), pp. 101 ff.

[19] Holzinger, *op. cit.,* chap. iv; and Lindquist, *A First Course,* chap. iv.

Usually, it is not sufficient merely to issue a written report of results. There should be an oral report to the faculty in large or small groups and conferences with individual members who wish to pursue some interpretation or to raise questions not treated in the report. It is at this stage that the best opportunity to affect the educational process presents itself. What can be accomplished will depend on the training and insight of the supervising groups, the channels of communication available to them, and the amount of time they may be able to devote to the undertaking. But it is essential that the number and kinds of programs undertaken be realistic in terms of the staff and the resources available.

A well-conceived and -administered evaluation plan, even though of modest dimension, cannot fail to be helpful to an institution and its students. At the same time it may prove to be the opening wedge for needed evaluations of other aspects of the institution. If these are equally well planned, patterns of procedure can be established in time that will make each new evaluation project more effective.

PART II

Descriptions of Selected College and
University Testing Programs

Introduction

IN THE DESCRIPTIONS OF SEVEN PROGRAMS OF TESTING WHICH FOL-
low, there is much that illustrates points made in the foregoing
pages. Each contribution, however, was written independently of
the main text, and their relationships, therefore, are somewhat
coincidental.

Some of these programs have developed over a long period of
years and some are relatively young. A variety of forms of organization for the administration of testing programs is represented. Of particular interest are the descriptions in each of how
tests are used to implement different aspects of its educational
planning. While all use tests to serve certain purposes, such as
admissions and placement, the fact that they use different kinds
of tests to do this and the variety of ways in which each operates
in the use of tests beyond these purposes reflect a versatility which
it was thought would be provocative.

The presentations are from institutions of different types of
organization and of different-sized enrollments. Among them will
be found descriptions of the programs conducted at a small private Eastern liberal arts college for women (Chatham College);
a coeducational liberal arts college within a large private Midwestern university (University of Chicago); a larger private Eastern liberal arts college for men (Dartmouth College); a coeducational college of liberal arts within a municipally supported university (University of Louisville); the program of a counseling
center of a very large Midwestern state university (University of
Minnesota); and the programs of two Western institutions, one a
large city-supported public junior college (Pasadena Junior College), and one a state-supported college of liberal arts (San Francisco State College).

8. The Testing Program of Chatham College

LILY DETCHEN, *Director of Evaluation Services*

RELATIVELY FEW SMALL COLLEGES MAINTAIN OFFICES THAT ENGAGE in comprehensive evaluation activities, chiefly because most such institutions believe that they cannot afford these services. This point of view is unfortunate, for it is not difficult to demonstrate that in the long run the provision of evaluation services is economically sound. Such an office can assist a faculty in their instructional responsibilities; a better instructional impact generally means better satisfied students and a higher retention rate. The selection of students who are scholastically able and eager is in itself an economy, considering the time and energy consumed by recruiting and retention activities in most private colleges. The provision of data that facilitate initial approaches to students and that assist with plans for their academic and general welfare surely represents an economy of effort for the staff and a more comfortable state of mind for a student, eliminating, as it can, many false moves on repetitious courses, placement at a wrong level, too heavy or too light an academic load, and so on. If evaluation activities accounted annually for the retention of only six students who might otherwise quietly fold their tents and slip away, they pay their way.

Not only can the small college afford such an activity, but indeed it should and must afford it, for this may mean its survival. The administrator of the smaller college who thinks he cannot "afford" the continual, systematic study and review of his college program and student body, entailing necessarily some physical facilities and a professional staff member to plan with him and his faculty, is not only maintaining a static educational program but also is foolishly losing students and, hence, income. Such a program can have its finest opportunity in the smaller college.

While it is granted that the large university can do many things better because it does have more specialists, the most comprehensive, useful, and personal interpretations are possible, I venture to say, in the informal, relaxed, and administratively uncluttered atmosphere of the smaller institution, provided that institution wishes to help its students to that degree.

Chatham College is a small liberal arts college of approximately 450 students and 65 full-time-equivalent faculty and administrative staff. During the past decade the college has instituted a series of curricular changes. It has been deemed important to maintain an analytical climate in respect to them, and simultaneously to keep planning abreast of the best research and evaluation practices. The Office of Evaluation Services was established ten years ago to assist in analyses of the curricular changes that were being introduced at that time and to promote a spirit of inquiry about the total educational venture. It is not our purpose to discuss here the total evaluation program at Chatham College but rather the current uses that it makes of tests and relevant considerations.

At Chatham the staff for this activity consists of a director trained in evaluation, a secretary-assistant with no previous technical training in testing, and twenty-five hours weekly of student clerical aid. Occasional examiner assistance is recruited from the admissions staff and a clerical allowance of $200 permits some extra occasional help. An IBM scoring machine and an electric calculator are necessary to the operations. Except during Freshman Week, no more is undertaken than can be handled by the office staff. It should be mentioned that the reproduction of examination copy, a sizable item, is managed by another unit. The office occupies a 20-by-27-foot area, including built-in closets for storing tests, and is glass-partitioned into three units. Adjacency to other administrative offices gives easy access to student records; location in the principal classroom and teacher-office building increases its efficiency and accessibility; a nearby conference room is available. Annual operating cost is about $11,000 for 450 students; there should be but small increase in cost for as many as 600 students. Expenses are borne by the office budget; none are charged against departmental or other special budgets but are considered as part of the total instruction budget for the college.

The selection of tests for the Chatham program may be influenced in any particular instance by several factors. A primary consideration is that no more tests are administered than can be utilized in terms of purposes and staff. Some tests are chosen, not because they are the very best instruments available in that area, but because they complement economically some other examination also being used. For example, someone reviewing the list might ask why a more diagnostic reading test is not included. Earlier such a test was used. More recently this has not been done because the current opinion is that, in the face of other needs, reading difficulties among our rather select group of students are not sufficiently prevalent to justify the employment of a reading expert, and until such time as we think they are, diagnostic reading testing is wasteful. It is much more important that we know whether students can, under the more reasonable and generous time allowances that duplicate their study and examination conditions, do analytical and interpretational reading, with accurate comprehension of material of standard difficulty. Testing for that objective is emphasized, and several tests of varied subject content, which also serve additional purposes, are used to obtain that information.

We also like to include some tests which do not impose rigorous time limits. While superior students may be expected to perform well under speeded conditions, some quite able students do not concentrate to the best of their ability under pressure. Since our college course examination periods are generous and, we hope, relaxed, there seems to be more sense in judging the performance of students tested under more leisurely conditions.

Sometimes we select and use an examination more for the purpose of an over-all appraisal of a group than for the appraisal of individuals in the group. The performance of all freshmen on an aptitude test that has been administered to them locally under uniform conditions of motivation and environment provides a gauge that has many general research and evaluation uses. We like, therefore, to supplement the required College Board Scholastic

Aptitude Tests with such an administration, and we use the School and College Ability Tests for the purpose.

Frequently, it is necessary to weigh the substitution of a new and somewhat better examination for one that has had several years of use in our own college and the performance of which, therefore, we already understand. We then introduce the new test but retain temporarily some of our regular battery until we establish the validity (for us) of the newer instrument.

Also, we bear in mind that no test is equally suited to all students, varying as they do in quality; administration time requirements, if nothing else, prohibit the publication of examinations with such comprehensive validity and reliability. For example, we have found that, of the tests we use, the American Council Psychological Examination, the Scholastic Aptitude Test, or the School and College Ability Tests will do a better job of identifying the brightest in our groups than will the high school level General Educational Development social studies test, which is more useful for identifying the academically weaker student.

Where there is an interest only in a rough screening of students, which occurs when we sift for those students who should try exemption examinations, we use brief examinations in preference to more time-consuming ones of higher statistical reliability and discriminatory validity. Provided we place our cutting points properly, we know that we have culled a group which will contain the students we really want to identify. To find eight students, say, we may have to subject twenty-five to a rigorous examination session, but one hundred and twenty-five can be excused.

Above all, we keep in mind that while a student cannot perform better in a test than she really is, her performance at a given time may not show her real attainment; she may have emotional instabilities that loom at test times, or be temporarily distracted by illness or problems, or not be motivated to do well. Therefore, for some individuals it is well to use a number of examinations administered at different times, with follow-up testing in questionable instances. For example, for most of our applicants we receive, from their high school, records of several IQ testings—along with records on other achievement tests obtained at different ages. In addition we have a College Board SAT and Achievement Tests report. These may all be well correlated, roughly, with the high school grade record. If so, we can rejoice and proceed with evaluation in earnest. But when there is a serious disagreement among some of these data, the applicant is retested either at the college or at the high school. No fixed set of tests is utilized; we select those tests that seem to cover best the applicant's preparation or that help resolve the discrepancy in the data already at hand. We may thereby salvage annually as many as ten desirable students who might otherwise be rejected. In this process, we select tests that we believe can be administered by someone relatively inexperienced in giving tests.

There are other considerations, but the above serves to illustrate the point that tests cannot be blindly accepted or naïvely categorized. Even the tests of the most reputable research teams have limitations in a given situation. Do not misunderstand me. I consider testing to be an invaluable tool. But there are few, if any, tests with built-in, ready-made solutions. The acceptance of the role of testing is, in general, threatened, not so much by testing instruments that claim to do what they do not do, as by persons who hope that they can do what they cannot, because life would be so much simpler if one could but accept the infallibility of testing. Judiciously used—and this means a balancing with still other tests and other relevant factors—tests certainly help in the formulation of reasonable approaches to some of the problems that arise with students. The role of the interpreter, however, is strategic.

KINDS OF TESTS USED

With some of the foregoing considerations and reservations in mind to help account for our selection of some one test over another, I will now describe the purposes for which we use tests and give the titles of tests currently in use.

Scholarship examinations

We have the usual problem of the small private college in most wisely dispensing the generous, but always inadequate, scholarship funds. We observe a graduated scale of grants, and naturally we want our larger awards to go to the most able of those who can make best use of assistance. We utilize the scholarship application form and data-collecting service provided by the Educational Testing Service, but the Admissions Office staff makes the final interpretation of need. Personal interviews are held with all applicants.

Earlier, most Chatham applicants were Pennsylvanians. Originally, this group was tested at the college in the spring. To them we gave such tests as the Iowa High School Content Examination and the Test of Critical Thinking.[1] As the radius of applicant clientèle broadened in accordance with a new emphasis in the admissions program, the testing of applicants at the college became increasingly difficult. Therefore, in 1954 Chatham began to require that scholarship applicants take the College Board Scholastic Aptitude Tests and three of the CEEB Achievement Tests, one in English and the other two of the applicant's choice. It continues to use the locally administered tests mentioned above in a few instances of late "deciders."

I might add, to further complicate this story, that some of our scholarship applicants have been taking neither our own scholarship battery nor the College Board battery, but the American Council Psychological Examination and an achievement examination developed especially for a county scholarship testing program. Since competition in the latter is high, we know that students in the top third of the group are exceptionally able. Therefore, when our applicants come from the high end of that distribution, we seldom need to test further.

This means, then, that when we begin to assign funds we may have a group of applicants with three separate kinds of test data—a situation less complicated than it seems. With a large pool of able students adequately identified by any of these methods, recommendations, other personal qualifications, and need become the final weights in decision-making.

[1] The Test of Critical Thinking, Form G, and the Test of Science Reasoning and Understanding were developed by the Cooperative Study of Evaluation in General Education of the American Council on Education. For availability, write to Educational Testing Service, 20 Nassau St., Princeton, N.J. For a list of the Study tests and inventories deposited with the ETS, see Paul L. Dressel and Lewis B. Mayhew, *General Education: Explorations in Evaluation* (Washington: The Council, 1954), Appendix I, p. 287.

Admissions Tests

With increases in tuition and a corresponding increase in number of scholarship applications, with extension of our geographic borders which makes local pretesting infeasible, with an increased demand from other colleges that applicants in whom we share interest take the CEEB Scholastic Aptitude Tests, and with our own long-established policy of requiring the Scholastic Aptitude Tests not only of scholarship applicants but of doubtful candidates, we were finding by 1954 that three-fourths of our applicants had already taken the Scholastic Aptitude Tests, and we knew, too, that having that measure for them in advance frequently was most useful. Therefore, it was inevitable that we should become one of the colleges requiring the Scholastic Aptitude Tests of all applicants. This occurred in 1956. With the entrants of 1958 we also began to require of all applicants three College Board Achievement Examinations. One of these is English and the other two are of the student's choice.

We continue to use other tests in admissions. There is always the student who failed to get to the examination center and in whom we are interested anyway! (And there is still an occasional high school that never heard of the College Boards!) While the large majority of admissions cases are clear-cut, with data and recommendations consistent enough to inspire confident decisions, as many as a fourth of the cases show warning signals which experience has taught us to heed. We watch for conflicts among grades, IQ's, the various IQ's when more than one IQ test has been used, College Board examination reports, independent high school testing reports, Regents Examinations reports, state-wide testing reports, and so on. The most frequent conflict is that between grades and examination data, with the latter lower. In such cases, we make further inquiry and frequently require further testing. Retesting in an "easier" environment with nonspeeded tests occasionally explains away a discrepancy between a good high school record and a poor examination performance. (I venture that this is true for one out of five retest cases.) The applicant is tested at the college, when that is possible, or a selection of tests is sent to a school or college for her. What is sent varies with the case, but usually we send several tests from the following list: the Test of

Critical Thinking, the Test of Science Reasoning and Understanding, two of the USAFI Tests of General Educational Development (Interpretation of Reading Materials in the Social Studies [high school] and Correctness and Effectiveness of Expression [college]), the Iowa High School Content Examination, the Nelson-Denny Reading Test, and the Cooperative General Culture Test (for transfer students only). On most of these tests, the college has its own norms based on the performance of six to twelve entering freshman classes.

The tests which are given to all freshmen at entrance serve the following purposes:

1. Describe the student for general purposes of immediate academic advising and sometimes for later advising in helping her make decisions;

2. Inform faculty members about the general caliber of students that the college receives and the caliber of students who eventually enter their particular courses or major areas;

3. Provide the several counseling deans and faculty counselors to students with general estimates of students, so that they have a more complete understanding of the capacity of any student with whom they may have special dealings (for example, they might or might not encourage a student to assume heavy work in leadership responsibilities with such evidence at hand);

4. Screen those students who will be given an opportunity to try for exemption from certain required courses;

5. Decide on best placement in foreign language and mathematics courses; and

6. Occasionally, with later posttesting, determine the gains made by the group in some subject.

With so many purposes to be served, and with the time available generous but never quite what is needed, we have had to trim test use closely. The present required entrance tests include: the School and College Ability Tests (only recently replacing the ACE Psychological Examination); the two GED tests, Interpretation of Reading Materials in the Social Studies (high school), and Correctness and Effectiveness of Expression (college)[2]; the Nelson-

[2] Available from the Veterans' Testing Service of the American Council on Education, 1785 Massachusetts Ave., N.W., Washington, D.C.

Denny Reading Test; the Test of Science Reasoning and Understanding; the Test of Critical Thinking, the Cooperative Foreign Languages Tests, the Cooperative Intermediate Algebra Test, and a locally constructed, brief exemption screening test related to a freshman course, Human Development and Behavior, for which no published test is available.

The results for the first five tests named above are listed and reported in "profile" form to faculty advisers and deans, with all faculty also receiving percentile score lists. The results for the remaining examinations, such as the foreign language examinations, go only to the faculty concerned. These items are delivered prior to the first registration.

Exemption examinations

The exemption examinations, for those subjects in the required basic curriculum from which the student may be exempted if she meets the standards, are locally constructed and are tailored to the specific course objectives. Those in freshman subjects are taken at the time of first entrance, the remaining ones in later years. Of the tests listed above, we use the GED test, Correctness and Effectiveness of Expression,[3] to screen those students who are to try the English composition exemption examination, which is locally prepared. The GED test, Interpretation of Reading Materials in the Social Studies, screens for both History of Western Civilization and Problems of Modern Society, with distribution of high school units in history also a consideration for selection for that examination. The history and social sciences exemption examinations are locally constructed, although they have been supplemented from time to time with such standardized examinations as the related portions of the Cooperative General Culture Test, the General Educational Development college-level social studies examination, and the Test of Critical Thinking in Social Science. For the course in Human Development and Behavior we use both a screening and an exemption examination which are locally constructed. It is estimated that in a class of 150 students there occur in all subjects

[3] In 1959 we may be able to replace this examination in our battery with the College Board Achievement Test in English.

about 75 screenings and 25 successful exemptions, excluding foreign language exemptions, in which approximately 30 percent of the group qualify at the required two-college-year standard.

There is under review, currently, a policy for accepting in lieu of some of our exemption examinations the results for those Advanced Placement Examinations of the College Entrance Examination Board which are pertinent to our basic curriculum requirements.

Course tests

Although occasionally an instructor may wish to give some published test in one of his courses, this is exceptional. Standardized tests seem to have a way of simply not fitting; or, when they do fit, the norms are completely unsuitable. Generally, the needed kind of course examination simply does not exist; the few that bear titles similar to the course either do not cover the objectives of the course or else they are weighted differently. This is true both of college courses in general education and of courses that are traditionally of the college content type.

For the most part, then, instructors write their own examinations, although they may borrow heavily, with the proper permission, from the examinations of friends located in other colleges and universities. A welcome recent development under the sponsorship of the Educational Testing Service has been the collection and cataloging of college test questions, which may be made available gradually by subjects in bound volumes. Just one of these catalogues, in the natural sciences, is now ready.[4] The idea is that any instructor may select ready-made questions to suit his own teaching objectives and emphases. The Office of Evaluation Services helps any instructor or group that is interested to set up examinations and to analyze them after administration. When registration supplies the necessary populations, the best of the material from examinations in the general education courses is culled for future use with new materials, which are, in turn, analyzed. It is a more or less continuous process of sowing, reaping, and sorting.

[4] Paul L. Dressel and Clarence H. Nelson, *Questions and Problems in Science: Test Item Folio No. 1* (Princeton, N.J.: Educational Testing Service, 1957).

General examinations

There are batteries of examinations which can be used to evaluate achievement in very broad terms for some major objectives of general education. We have used such batteries from time to time and will undoubtedly continue to do so. I refer to such batteries as the National College Sophomore Testing Program, the Graduate Record Area Examinations, the Tests of General Educational Development, and the less well known and not too generally available tests and inventories of the Cooperative Study of Evaluation in General Education of the American Council on Education, which stresses critical thinking skills. A college which is interested in a general self-evaluation may want to make use of each one of these batteries at different times, since each series has an individual and important validity and a different quality of student and type of institution represented in its norms.

TESTING FOR SOME SPECIAL PURPOSES

Besides these regular functions of testing at Chatham, other special applications of tests are made. Our college sometimes considers the application of a student who has not been graduated formally from high school, but who, nevertheless, seems ready for college and wishes to enter. We have been admitting one or two such students each year for about ten years. Occasionally an applicant has taken a commercial program in high school, but finds it possible and desirable at the end of her senior year to attend college. Occasionally some older applicant wants to enter, but, after her long absence from study, lacks the confidence to do so. Testing is helpful in all of these cases. We have sent tests for students in foreign countries, not so much to decide whether or not to accept them, for such students usually have been highly recommended, as to know how fast they may be expected to adjust academically and what kind of initial program is feasible. When transfer students offer preparation for which it is difficult to determine equivalence, we can often, through testing, do a better job of credit evaluation. We have used tests to evaluate the preparation of any student who has come to us with a background that we did not fully understand, for example, a blind student who completed a secondary school training program in a specialized school for the blind, and several young students from other countries who had had only one year of high school in the United States.

It cannot be overemphasized that we do not formulate decisions completely on test results in such cases, but they do help immensely. In all these instances, we use, whenever we can, examinations which we have already used for regular purposes and for which we have developed norms; but they may not always be suitable, so we sometimes turn to other measures. We keep a fairly large stock of sample copies of all the Cooperative tests and Form B, USAFI subject examinations. Of course, we also consider carefully any previous test records that exist for the student, writing for them if the student tells us that she has taken tests.

INDIVIDUAL GUIDANCE USES

Scarcely a day passes when the test records on file in our office are not utilized for at least several students. At certain times (when students are declaring majors, when course grades are due, and so on) the incidence is higher. Although reports are sent to all faculty members so that they may make their own general interpretations of the test scores, many prefer to verify their conclusions at the office. Even the more experienced staff counselors do so. The types of questions that come up are of considerable variety; generally, they are of some such nature as these:

Joan is not participating in class discussion; nothing seems to interest her. I feel that I may be getting nowhere with her. Is the trouble with me or with the student?

Nancy wants to reduce her seventeen-hour program to fourteen hours because she says she can't keep up with her assignments. Should I encourage her to do so?

Ruth's family has had financial reverses and she may have to withdraw from college unless we offer scholarship aid. How much of our emergency funds can we justify for this student in terms of what we have done for others of the same potential?

Loretta has a sinus condition which is causing frequent absences. Her family is trying to decide whether she should withdraw from college or whether she will be able to continue with frequent absences. Does it seem that she could carry on independently?

Betty wants to work six hours a week in the dining room. She is already working Saturdays off-campus. We don't think she needs the money, but we need the service. Should she be encouraged to do this?

Judy wants to study French privately this summer and try to exempt her language requirement in the fall. Is this advisable?

Susan wants to enter a graduate school which requires the Graduate Record Area Examinations. Is she likely to do well in those examinations?

Joanne is making the lowest grade in the class. Can she be expected to do better?

Catherine is being considered as an editor of the yearbook. Should she be encouraged to seek this appointment, which is very time-consuming?

Dorothy has been good in my classes except that she cannot meet my standards of English proficiency in her written work. Why? Doesn't she know better, or is this a case of carelessness?

Gladys is being considered for a job by a local industry. Can you provide any statement of her test records that may be helpful to her in securing the job to send along with her other records?

I wish to emphasize that in none of these situations is an answer automatically supplied by tests; but the combination of test results, other information, and the special insights of those persons most concerned merge to clarify the problem and find a solution.

EDUCATIONAL RESEARCH STUDIES

Test records of students are kept readily available so that problems that arise in relation to the program in general may be studied. Some sample kinds of general questions that tests have helped us to resolve have been: Do certain admissions policies operate to improve the quality of candidates? Are students who enter the education program as able as other student groups? Are grading standards of the college, its departments, and its individual instructors reasonably fair? What caliber of students transfer? How well does our education curriculum, developed after much controversy, prepare students? How may a class be divided into units of fairly equal caliber for experimental instructional purposes? How do students of different caliber fare under different instructional organization or methods? Which high schools may regularly be depended upon to refer acceptable applicants to us; which, inferior applicants? (The latter obviously do not understand our standards and need enlightenment.) Is student performance in the general education program the equivalent of normal expectation in other liberal arts colleges? Are there unequal achievements by areas to be resolved? Does work in certain courses stimulate students to keep abreast of current affairs? Who are the underachievers among students? Does the relatively heavy emphasis in general education affect achievement adversely in the field of the major? Or does it support the major?

The above questions have actually arisen in the past year or two. Each year will bring new ones. Most of these are reported on directly to the originating group, but all are briefly reported to all faculty in a bulletin issued periodically by the office. Faculty also receive lists of the results of any tests that may be given to students, along with appropriate instruction for interpretation. A *Faculty Handbook* also carries a dozen pages or more describing the general functions and services of the office, chiefly for the benefit of new faculty. Not all of these services are test-centered and hence not all have been described here.

To summarize:
1. Tests are useful and important in conscientious educational planning;
2. Tests must be taken with a grain of salt—no test is infallible;
3. The administration of many tests and the processing of much test data are meaningless and expensive routines unless the results are put to work for the individual and for the total program;
4. Test interpretations cannot exist in a vacuum, but must be utilized differently and varied with the kind of decision that is pending;
5. A testing program is not the prerogative of the larger institution, but is just as much needed, and eminently more flexible, in the smaller institution.

9. The Testing Program of the College of the University of Chicago

CHRISTINE McGUIRE, *Examiner in the Social Sciences*

EACH YEAR THE COLLEGE OF THE UNIVERSITY OF CHICAGO EN-rolls some five hundred entering students in a variety of four-year programs, each leading to the A.B. or B.S. degree. The student's choice of program is, of course, dependent on his academic and professional interests. But all programs are alike in that each consists of two major components: general education and specialized education. Both the length and content of the specialized education component vary with the demands of the student's field of interest, as is common in most colleges and universities. In general, these requirements are determined primarily by the appropriate academic department. However, it may be interesting to note that though the purpose of the general education component is the same for all students, namely, "to give a common, critical understanding of the major fields of human knowledge and their interrelationships," both the length and content of that particular part of the students' education may also vary, depending on: (1) their previous education and (2) their chosen fields of specialization.

The following remarks about the testing program at the University of Chicago refer primarily to the techniques for establishing and for satisfying these general education requirements of the undergraduate curriculum. The system in its present form has evolved from the set of curriculum reforms initiated in 1931. At that time a series of integrated general courses was substituted for the existing elementary departmental offerings and the A.B. was redefined to require each candidate for the degree to develop certain broad understanding and skill in each of the major fields of knowledge. These revisions in the curriculum were accompanied by sweeping changes in traditional educational practices. These latter were designed to implement a plan of giving greater independence to students of exceptional ability by freeing them from all requirements of course credit, class attendance, daily and weekly assignments, and the like. All students were encouraged, but were not required, to attend lectures and class discussions, to submit for criticism written or laboratory work, or to study more or less independently. By the same action the instructional staff was relieved of the onerous roles of disciplinarian and judge and was freed to devote more effort and attention to its teaching duties.

It soon became clear that as a by-product of this release of both students and teachers for the pursuit of more appropriate educational purposes, grades and teachers' opinions of students could no longer be used to enforce attendance or coerce particular work and study habits. It was hoped that, as a result, students would be moved by more appropriate motives in selecting the particular educational experiences in which they elected to participate. For the realization of these aspirations, it was felt essential to substitute a system of comprehensive examinations covering a year's work in each broad field for the usual devices of course grades and credits.

An Office of the University Examiner, independent of the instructional staff, was therefore established. It was the function of this office to plan, construct, and administer[1] the various comprehensive examinations required in the general studies program, and on invitation to cooperate with other faculties in the university who desired its services on particular examination or evaluation programs. A board of examiners composed of representatives from the several faculties was established to determine the general policies of the Office of the University Examiner. Responsibility for specific policy with respect to particular comprehensive examinations was divided between the instructional staff in the relevant general courses and the examiner. The instructional staff was to be solely responsible for determining the objectives of each general course, and the examiner was charged with the technical job of

---

[1] Subsequently, responsibility for the actual administration of all examinations has been placed in a separate Office of Test Administration.

designing test exercises which would measure student achievement of these objectives, of grading the examinations, and of certifying the results to the registrar.[2]

The theory of the testing program at the University of Chicago as it has developed from this early beginning can be briefly summarized as follows:

First, the program assumes that the evaluation of academic achievement of students is most reliable and valid if based directly on students' performance on tasks which demand that they demonstrate the knowledge, skills, and ability which are objectives of the curriculum.

Second, these evaluations are regarded as significantly more valid and reliable if they are made in such a way as to be independent of the student's relation to the instructor and even of such considerations as the length of time he has served or his diligence in performing assigned work.

Third, it appears that the more important objectives can be measured only in connection with substantial blocks of subject matter without heavy reliance on the recall of detailed factual information.

Fourth, it is felt that the more important objectives can be measured only if the student is required to apply his knowledge and skills to new problems.

Fifth, it is considered of basic importance that all testing and evaluation should be closely related to teaching and curricular problems and should be utilized to guide both students and instructors in the planning of their educational experience.

KINDS OF TESTS USED

On the basis of these principles the testing program at the level of general education has gradually been extended to include four major types of tests: scholastic aptitude tests, tests of previous academic achievement, advisory achievement tests to inform the student and the instructional staff about the student's progress to-

[2] Since the initial preparation of this manuscript, the administrative structure in which the examiners in the general education program operate has been modified. The legislative and budgetary changes involved in this reorganization have not, I believe, influenced the principles employed by these examiners or the general practices which will be described.

ward the objectives of the program, and final comprehensive examinations of achievement in particular parts of the general education curriculum. The tests themselves, their major purposes, and the uses made of their results are described below.

Entrance examinations

Applicants for admission to the University of Chicago are required to take an entrance or scholarship examination which is designed to provide evidence about the candidate's ability to do academic work at the level required in the College of the University of Chicago or in the division to which the student is applying. At present, this entrance and scholarship battery consists of the Scholastic Aptitude Test of the College Entrance Examination Board,[3] a test of reading comprehension, and a test of skill in quantitative reasoning. All tests except the first are composed locally by the Office of the University Examiner.

All entrance tests are designed to help answer the question: Does this particular student have a reasonable chance of succeeding in the University of Chicago program considering the expected level and pace of work and the nature and conditions of instruction offered? In the case of the scholarship applicant, the question becomes: Does this particular student have a reasonable prospect of doing more than satisfactory, perhaps even distinguished, work in this type of program? Hence, the tests are designed to give evidence about the specific abilities needed to meet the demands of this particular program.

To illustrate: The program stresses the importance of dealing directly with primary source materials. Students are normally expected to use original sources rather than to rely on reading about such documents. As a result there is a substantial amount of reading in the undergraduate program which places a premium on the experience that students can use in its interpretation. In the classroom, there is almost no lecturing or quizzing about this reading. Rather it is expected that students will be able to participate in a group attack on a common problem and to discuss intelligently the nature and ideas of the various documents considered.

[3] Candidates from local high schools are permitted to substitute the American Council Psychological Examination for a part of this battery.

It is important, therefore, that the reading comprehension test be one on the basis of which we can predict whether or not students will be able to share in and profit from such discussions. Consequently, the reading test is neither a measure of reading speed, nor of simple understanding of the words or sentences, but is rather a test of the ability to deal with ideas presented in short passages representative of various styles and subjects. Other components of the entrance test battery are designed on the basis of similar types of considerations.

One other set of issues has been important in determining the design of entrance tests. Often colleges and universities have been criticized on the ground that their admission policies have tended to place serious limitations on secondary school curricula. The University of Chicago has made a deliberate effort to establish admission criteria and to develop tests which identify students with the appropriate intellectual qualifications without penalizing those whose high school experience is unconventional and without imposing a pattern of rigid requirements that high schools feel obligated to meet.

The tests currently employed reflect both policy and technical decisions reached as the outcome of long discussions carried on between members of the Examiner's Office and of the College faculty. The latter is represented by various committees concerned with problems of admissions which, in combination with the Office of Admissions, determine the university's policy at the undergraduate level. In the establishment of this policy the university examiner is provided with a list of the intellectual qualities on which it would be desirable to have evidence about applicants. The university examiner is then responsible for devising techniques to assess prospective entrants with respect to these qualities. The resulting exercises are often reviewed and criticized by relevant policy groups to be sure that they measure at the appropriate level the kinds of aptitudes which actually ought to be important in determining admission to the university.

Test results for each applicant, together with interpretive data, are made available to the Office of Admissions and to student advisers by the Examiner's Office. The latter has no power to make a decision about an applicant but, in reporting the level and pattern of scores for each prospective student, identifies those suggestive of probable failure in the program or those which suggest the desirability of various types of remedial action, prior to or concurrent with the student's first year in the program. For instance, in borderline cases remedial reading and/or writing programs may be recommended for some students. Cases requiring other special action are often drawn to the attention of the Admission's Office or adviser's office. It should perhaps be stressed that no single criterion is by itself critical in determining an applicant's admissibility to the university. Rather the constellation of a student's scores is considered, together with information from interviews and other data about him. These data as now employed assist the Office of Admissions in selecting students who are likely to complete successfully the requirements of the particular parts of the university to which they are applying.

Placement tests

It should be obvious from the above discussion that the entrance test results are widely used by advisers and are available to faculty for the purpose of advising the student about his program, but never for the purpose of determining his requirements once he has been admitted. The tests which we are about to describe can be said to have almost the reverse function: they are used primarily to determine the student's general education requirements and only secondarily to advise him regarding the best means of meeting those requirements.

It may be necessary at this point to describe briefly the general education component of the undergraduate curriculum in order to make clear the way in which the placement tests function. The total offering of general education from which a student's requirements are selected consists of three, three-year sequences: one each in social sciences, humanities, and natural sciences; a one-year sequence each in mathematics, English, and foreign language; and two additional one-year sequences, one organized on historical principles and the other on philosophical principles, designed to assist the student in achieving an integrated view of his educational experiences. As stated above, the student's general education requirements are determined from among these fourteen general courses on the basis of his previous academic achievement and his plans for future specialization. It is in the determination of his previous academic achievement that the placement testing program at the university is relevant. A student is not able to satisfy requirements in the general studies program by presenting credits for satisfactory work done in related courses in high school or other colleges. Rather he must demonstrate that he has achieved a minimum level of competence in the required area. He can demonstrate his competence in only two ways: (1) on placement tests taken during the first week of his attendance at the university or (2) on comprehensive examinations covering the required course and offered twice yearly, at the end of the spring and summer terms.[4]

Each entering student is given placement tests of achievement in each major field and is excused from any part (or all) of the general education component of the bachelor's program in which his scores indicate that he has already achieved the minimun required level of knowledge, skill, and ability. It should be noted that contrary to the practice in many schools and colleges, the placement tests are not designed to answer such questions as: Would the student profit from a year's instruction in the beginning course? Is the student ready to take the next highest course in a sequence? At what level should he be placed in order to perform best in a given sequence?

The one question which the placement tests are designed to answer is: Has the student already achieved, irrespective of his previous formal education, the objectives of this sequence at the required minimum level?[5] This approach necessitates the development of tests which give the student an opportunity to demonstrate all the important knowledge and skills which are regarded by the faculty as the essential objectives of a particular general

[4] This policy is currently undergoing a revision which permits transfer students to substitute for the relevant examinations credit earned at other colleges when such credit represents work of the appropriate quantity and quality. A similar modification of the policy is under consideration which would permit high school graduates to offer the Advanced Placement Tests prepared by the College Entrance Examination Board for limited credit.

[5] However, to the extent that the general education courses are actually logically and psychologically sequential, placement on the basis of this criterion would yield results similar to those obtained from answers to the two previous questions.

course. At the same time, the test items must be independent of specific reading lists and of specialized terminology which is not in itself essential to the objectives of the course. The tests must be independent even of those concepts and approaches to a field which may be peculiar to a particular course, faculty, or series of readings and, hence, parochial in the sense that they are not generally familiar to people who are well informed and competent in the field.

As is apparent from the above discussion, the knowledge, skills, and abilities which should be sampled in any placement test are determined by the objectives of the relevant course. The College faculty generally, and specifically the staff responsible for a particular general course, determines the objectives which constitute the basic specifications of a placement test. Ordinarily these specifications are so formulated that they identify both the skills a student is expected to develop and the content or problem areas to which he should be able to apply these skills. It is then the duty of the Office of the University Examiner to design tests which are valid in measuring student achievement in the designated respects and which are at the same time appropriate for students who represent a wide variety of previous educational experience.

In principle, the system described here implies a sharp separation of responsibilities: the policy decisions to be made by the relevant faculties or course staffs and the technical implementation of those policies to be accomplished by the Examiner's Office. In practice, however, these administratively independent groups cooperate fully both in the determination of objectives and in their implementation in the testing program.[6] The examiner in a given subject is also engaged in some teaching duties on the staff for which he is examiner and both formally and informally works closely with that staff. He often finds it necessary, for instance, to stimulate the staff to revise or reformulate its objectives so as to make them sufficiently specific for test and evaluation purposes. He frequently finds that in faculty discussion of specific test materials objectives are clarified and, at the same time, new devices for measuring them are suggested. Similarly staff criticism of test materials

[6] The interdependence of the instructional and examining functions was recognized explicitly in the administrative reorganization referred to above.

is considered in revising and editing, not only specific items, but also, on occasion, the general nature of an entire test. Alternatively, data reported to the relevant staffs concerning initial student competence and deficiencies are utilized in the revision of course materials. Finally, the standards for excusing students from a particular general course are worked out jointly by the Examiner's Office and the appropriate teaching staff.

Since, as indicated above, the primary function of the placement test is to determine whether or not a student has already achieved the objectives of a given general education course, it may be interesting to note how the data about student performance are used in determining each student's required program of general studies. Before a placement test is given to entering students, the items are tried out in the comprehensive examinations with regularly enrolled students who have just completed the general course. Their performance is used as the basis for establishing a level of satisfactory achievement, that is one which indicates that the major aims of the course have been achieved at the minimum desired level. If for some reason such a technique of pretesting is infeasible, other methods of establishing a satisfactory level of performance are employed. The scores of each entering student are compared with these pre-established standards and his performance is evaluated as indicating (1) that he has already acquired the necessary knowledge or skills and, hence, should be excused from the course; or (2) that he is considerably better prepared than the average student and, hence, should be able either to complete the course in less than the normal time or to take more than the normal load of courses; or (3) that his preparation is adequate, but not superior and, hence, he should be expected to devote the normal amount of time to completion of the course; or (4) that his preparation is inadequate and he should be given remedial or other extra instruction. Recommendations of the type described immediately above are made solely on the basis of the student's performance on the placement test and without reference to his previous education in the subject. As a result some students without formal courses in a subject-matter area may be excused from a given course, while others with records of extensive course work may be required to take a comprehensive examination in that field. The placement test scores together with the above evaluations and other data helpful in interpreting the scores are reported to the student's adviser, who uses them in combination with a consideration of the student's proposed field of specialization, as a basis for determining the student's required program of general studies and for advising him informally about the combined work-and-study load which he should undertake. The data are also available to any College staff or individual faculty member who may wish to know more about the composition of his current class or who may find such data helpful in informal conferences with students.

This program has had a three-fold result: (1) By placing students in courses that they need and are prepared to take and by encouraging them to progress as rapidly as possible, repetition of learning experiences has been minimized and student and faculty time is thereby economized. (2) By indicating what courses a student is prepared to study or what remedial work he needs, failure among students has been reduced. (3) By supplying the teaching staff with evidence about initial student status, it has been possible to redesign courses so that they are appropriate for the actual student body.

Advisory tests of student achievement

Once or twice during the first two quarters of a three-quarter course students are given the opportunity to take a number of test exercises under regular examination conditions. These exercises sample the work of the course to date and give the student an opportunity to demonstrate the extent to which he is acquiring the knowledge and skills regarded by the staff as important objectives of the course. The exercises are composed of questions which are similar to those the student will later encounter on the final comprehensive examination and are designed to serve both teaching and testing purposes. They are regarded as important educational experiences in that they, like the class discussion, help to orient the student and to inform him about the specific aims to which the course is dedicated; they presumably present him with challenging problems which encourage him to apply to new situations the knowledge and skills which he has been developing in the course; and by giving him experience with such exercises in an examination situation, it is hoped that tension and other obstacles arising from inexperience will be minimized in the final comprehensive examination. The exercises serve an evaluation purpose both for the student and the staff of a course: papers are scored and returned to each student with an indication of the quality of performance represented by his score. However, grades on these tests are purely advisory, do not form a part of the student's permanent academic record, and cannot be used as a means of establishing credit to meet a general education requirement. The instructional staff receives reports of individual scores for use in advising students with respect to their work. In addition, group responses to each item in the exercises are reported to the teaching staff for use in assessing the effectiveness of the current selection of readings and discussions in meeting the objectives of the course.

The instructional staff has always had the formal responsibility of planning, constructing, and administering these tests. However, since it is clearly recognized that to be of maximal value they should be based on the same principles as the comprehensive examination (which is the responsibility of the Examiner's Office), most staffs and examiners have followed the practice of joint planning and preparation of these test materials.

Comprehensive examinations of student achievement

Repeated reference has been made to the comprehensive examination. Initially the student's general education requirements are formulated in terms of the kinds of competence he should attain rather than the number of courses he must complete. This competence is measured by a series of comprehensive examinations. Each examination is usually six hours in length and is given at the end of each of the general education courses. The student's performance on these examinations is the sole criterion for determining his grades and for meeting his requirements for graduation. Unless a student is excused from a required course on the basis of his performance on the placement test,[7] he must pass the relevant comprehensive examination in order to meet his general studies requirements. The student is free to take an examination without formal registration or attendance in the course

[7] Or on the basis of appropriate transfer, as has been explained.

that would ordinarily prepare him for it, and he may repeat it as frequently as he wishes.

The system of comprehensive examinations is one of the oldest aspects of the testing program at the University of Chicago. When it was initiated, there was some concern about the ensuing division of responsibility between the faculty, who was expected to determine the objectives of the general courses, and the newly created Office of the University Examiner, which was to develop comprehensive examinations appropriate to these objectives. In some quarters it was feared that an independent office of examinations would soon dictate the curriculum and restrict instructional work to cram sessions for the final examination or, alternatively, that instructors would develop such detailed specifications of objectives that the resulting examinations would be merely course examinations, in no sense comprehensive. Neither of these dangers has actually materialized. The close cooperation between each instructional staff and the examiner in each field has obviated the first problem; at the same time, the existence of a group of individuals with common concerns in improving examinations and with the time and resources for experimentation in this area minimized difficulties of the latter sort.

From the joint effort of the instructional and the examining staffs a number of new types of testing techniques have gradually been developed which have influenced both examining and instructional practices. One of the most interesting is the extensive use of open-book examinations even with nonessay types of tests. Students are encouraged to bring any books and notes they may wish to use to the examination. The questions are designed to require the students to apply concepts and principles to new situations ranging from the analysis in the Humanities Comprehensive of an unfamiliar sonata or painting to the interpretation in the Natural Sciences Comprehensive of a scientific paper or report of an experiment new to the students and to the evaluation in the Social Sciences Comprehensive of specific governmental policies not discussed in the relevant course. This particular technique has required the Examiner's Office to develop analytical rather than informational types of objective questions and has freed instructional staffs from the necessity of covering a detailed body of subject matter and encouraged them to develop alternative modes of accomplishing the same broad objectives.

By this time it is probably clear that the comprehensives differ from the tests described in previous sections in a number of important respects. First, they differ from the entrance and scholarship tests in attempting to measure achievement in particular subjects rather than general scholastic aptitude. They differ from the placement tests in that all students who take them can be presumed to have at least one set of common educational experiences (that is, a common reading list); hence questions requiring a high level of analysis can be based on particular readings without fear that unfamiliarity with that specific book or author will constitute an unreasonable obstacle. They differ from the advisory tests, first, in that performance on them does form a part of the student's permanent record, and hence his interest in them may differ; and second, they cover such substantial areas of subject matter that it is feasible to require the student to demonstrate a level of analysis and integration that would be quite impossible in the quarterly advisory tests.

The characteristics of the comprehensives are reflected in the nature of the results obtained from them and the uses to which these results are put. Since the primary purpose of the examination is to certify the level of student achievement, standards of excellence for each examination are established jointly by the appropriate instructional staff and examiner. These standards are set on the basis of data from experience with previous examinations and in the light of prior criteria which the instructional staff has developed regarding its expectations about the desired quality of student performance. On the basis of these standards, individual student scores on the examination are translated into conventional letter grades which are reported to the registrar and to the student. In addition, the student is given a rather detailed description of the quality of his work on various categories of the examination. For this purpose, each item in the examination is classified with respect to the particular content which it samples and with respect to the type of skill or ability required to answer it correctly. The student is informed about his performance in each of these content and skill categories. Such reports were initially prepared only for students who made low grades on an examination, with the thought that such an analysis would be useful to anyone who needed or wished to repeat an examination. However, students whose work was clearly satisfactory began to request these reports so frequently, that they are now made to every student as a matter of routine.

Reports to the faculty of the results of comprehensive examinations have differed over the years and currently vary among the several examiners. The instructional staff has access to any of the data on comprehensive examinations which are obtained in the routine process of scoring papers and reporting student grades. In addition, the Examiner's Office supplies them with any special data they may request or find useful in curriculum consideration and revision. As a general rule, such data include a summary of group responses to each question in the examination, together with more or less extensive interpretations of and hypotheses about the results. These data and their interpretations are used in varying degrees by the several instructional staffs in considering curriculum revisions.

The Examiner's Office has been continually concerned with devising improved means of reporting examination data to maximize their usefulness to the faculty in evaluating the efficacy of alternative teaching materials and procedures. For instance, on certain occasions reports have been made comparing student performance on questions in placement tests with their performance on identical or parallel questions in comprehensives. Such data have been used as one source of evidence about the nature and amount of improvement in student skills and knowledge resulting from the related general course. On other occasions data about performance on different types of questions or in different content areas have been used as one source of information about the need for reorganization of course materials, or for strengthening certain aspects of the general education program. On other occasions performance of students in different types of programs have been compared. This method has been used in connection with consideration of variant forms of the general courses and has been used in evaluating the consequences of alternative placement procedures.

OTHER ASPECTS OF THE TESTING PROGRAM AT THE UNIVERSITY OF CHICAGO

The testing program described above is employed in the general studies part of the College curriculum. However, several of the divisions and professional schools also employ certain of these techniques with their students. Most departments and schools rely heavily on data from entrance tests in judging student applications for admission. In addition, since the university requires that a student have a broad general education before undertaking specialized work in the divisions or professional schools, tests of general education (a variant of the placement tests described above) are used in the divisions and professional schools to identify the students who have acquired a general education and to indicate the fields in which other students are deficient. A few departments have used comprehensive examinations in basic skill courses in the field of specialization. Many departments require candidates for advanced degrees to demonstrate a reading knowledge of one or more foreign languages; the competence is certified on the basis of tests offered by the Examiner's Office. Also that office has worked with many departments on special evaluation problems.

In addition, the Examiner's Office has frequently been invited to cooperate in broad evaluation or follow-up studies of graduates of the College. In these studies, it has been recognized that the effectiveness of the College can and should be measured in terms of many criteria other than the level of knowledge and skills it would be appropriate to test for in a comprehensive examination. Hence, some of these studies have focused on the long-term benefits of the College program, others on the attitudes and habits of College graduates, and still others on their opinions about many aspects of College and university life, both curricular and extracurricular.

Finally, both the Examiner's Office as a whole and individual examiners have participated in a wide variety of research and testing programs other than those described above. These have included curriculum and testing programs of other schools and universities and of various professional groups and research programs, including personality and assessment studies as well as those more directly related to the evaluation of patterns of intellectual and academic achievement.

The listing of the various activities carried on by the Examiner's Office suggests the variety of personnel currently included on the staff. When the Examiner's Office was first established, it was staffed primarily with professional psychologists who had specialized in the field of tests and measurement. The early work of the office reflected their primary concern with the development of improved techniques of measurement and the statistical evaluation of these new modes of testing. Many of the early research studies made substantial contributions to statistical theory and its application to test and measurement problems. More recently, the staff of the Examiner's Office has included a larger proportion of people whose initial specialization is in the subject in which they serve as examiners. As a result, both the research and writing done by members of the Examiner's Office now reflect their basic concern with scholarly problems in the field of their academic interest, issues of teaching and curriculum construction, as well as evaluation, and finally the interrelation of these various problems.

The development of the extensive testing and research program now carried on by the Examiner's Office was made possible by its establishment as an organization which, through cooperating closely with the instructional staff, had an identity and functions independent of the day-to-day problems of that staff. At the same time, members of the examiner's staff have found their work greatly facilitated by their association with and participation in college teaching. Similarly, the university testing program has itself been enriched by the challenging and stimulating association that members of the Examiner's Office have enjoyed in the many testing, evaluation, and research projects in which they participate outside the university.

10. The Testing Program of Dartmouth College

CLARK W. HORTON, *Consultant in Educational Research*

DARTMOUTH COLLEGE IS A PRIVATE FOUR-YEAR LIBERAL ARTS COL-
lege for men with a freshman class of about 725 and an undergraduate enrollment of about 2,800. It draws its students from all
over the United States with heaviest representation from the
Middle West, Middle Atlantic states, and New England. About
two-thirds of its students are from public high schools, one-third
from independent schools. Over 80 percent come from the top
quarter of their classes. Attrition in the first year is less than 4 percent; attrition before graduation less than 20 percent. The testing
program at Dartmouth has developed in response to needs for
information useful in admission, course placement and proficiency
exemption, guidance, and the evaluation of achievement in courses
of study.

ADMISSIONS TESTING

Beginning with the class of 1956 all applicants have been required to submit scores on the College Entrance Examination
Board Scholastic Aptitude Test. The afternoon program of
achievement tests is not required, although it is suggested to the
candidate that scores on such tests "are used, when available, for
placement, guidance, and proficiency exemption after matricula-
tion." About 60 percent of a class does take the afternoon program. The Dartmouth selective process utilizes a wide range of
information about the candidate, including: the quality of the
secondary school record; ratings and recommendations by the
school principal; rank in class; evidence of motivation, character,
and of breadth and depth of interests and achievements. In this

146

process the College Board scores play an important but not a determining role.

Some years ago the Educational Testing Service studied the value of important items of our preadmission data for predicting the first-year grade-point average and developed an index in which optimum weight is assigned to the SAT–Verbal score, the SAT–Mathematical score, rank in high school class, and the principal's recommendation as adjusted by the Admissions Office. This *predictive index* is computed for each applicant, and plays an important though not necessarily a determining role in admission decisions. Continuing studies of the validity of this index yield correlations of over .60 with the first-year and the two-year grade-point averages and of about .55 with the four-year average. The results of such studies are also expressed as experience tables, which serve as expectancy tables in guidance as well as in admissions.

FRESHMAN ORIENTATION

During Freshman Week entering students take a large battery of tests. In the fall of 1957 all men took Reading Comprehension, Test C2, and the Mechanics of Expression Test of the Cooperative English Test; the Strong Vocational Interest Blank; the Minnesota Multiphasic Personality Inventory; and a form prepared by the Office of Student Counseling to explore aspects of the student's personal history and his educational and vocational plans. Appropriate groups take placement and proficiency tests in a variety of subjects. All men enrolling for a foreign language course above the beginning level take a College Board Advanced Placement Test in that language. Selected groups take tests in American history, European history, mathematics, chemistry, physics, biology, and English. In some subjects, CEEB Advanced Placement Tests or other published tests are used; in others, the tests are objective tests developed by the departments. The latter frequently are tests that have been used as part of the final examination in the beginning course, sometimes over several years, and on which the scores made by large populations completing the course serve as normative data for the appropriate course placement or proficiency exemption of entering students. Under the auspices of the Thayer School of Engineering, one of the

Dartmouth Associated Schools, interested men take the Educational Testing Service Pre-Engineering Ability Test, and the results are used in counseling. Candidates for the Army, Navy, and Air Force ROTC units take qualifying tests administered by those units. All men have a thorough physical examination at entrance, and all men not medically excused take four physical ability tests developed by our Department of Physical Education.

The scores on all tests of general interest are put on punch cards, and converted to standard scores or percentiles in the tabulating center. Percentiles are based on the class itself, but tables of percentile norms on the population entering over the past several years are available for reference. Alphabetical lists of raw scores, standard scores, and percentiles are prepared in duplicate and placed in the hands of the Office of Student Counseling and the deans, together with appropriate profile sheets, tables of norms, and other aids in interpretation. Although there is a system of faculty advisers to foster closer student-faculty relations and to aid in academic guidance, the scores are not systematically made available to all advisers. Some who are interested and competent to interpret the scores get copies of the scores reports at their request. A current experiment in which six such advisers are leading discussion groups in connection with a required freshman course, The Individual and the College, offers promise of increased interest and competence in the use of test data by faculty advisers.

Scores on the C2 Reading Comprehension Test serve not only as supplementary evidence of academic potential and for diagnosis in counseling, but are also used to select the men to be invited, and to decide about others who seek permission, to participate in reading improvement groups. Such groups work through a semester on the improvement of reading skill and on study methods in general. About 35 percent of the freshmen complete this voluntary noncredit course; about 40 percent participate in at least part of it. A variety of reading tests, vocabulary tests, and locally made inventories of study habits, knowledge of examination techniques, and the like are used in this work.

The Strong Vocational Interest Blank is scored by a simplified method for the group scores and selected occupations. The most probable Strong standard scores derived from the simplified scores are reported, and these data are used in the Office of Student Counseling in conferences on the student's vocational plans and course choices. Several hundred freshmen seek such conferences. On request of the counselor the original paper may be scored for additional occupations. Some one hundred men retake the test in the junior or senior year, and their papers are scored for all occupations specified by the counselor. The Tuck School of Business Administration, two-year Associated School entered by some seventy-five Dartmouth students at the end of the junior year, administers the Strong test to its second-year men. The Minnesota Multiphasic Personality Inventory was used with the entire freshman class for the first time in the fall of 1957, and its value to us is under investigation.

Many tests are used with individual students or small groups in the work of the Office of Student Counseling, the tests used being determined by the nature of the problem. These tests include many titles in the categories: general intelligence or scholastic aptitude; achievement in academic subjects; tests of more specific aptitudes; tests of interest and personality. Other tests are used for experimental, demonstration, or guidance purposes in the classes of the Department of Psychology; for example, all students in Psychology 1, some 90 percent of each class, take the Allport-Vernon-Lindzey Study of Values.

PLACEMENT EXAMINATIONS

The most extensive, long-standing use of tests for placement and proficiency exemption is in the foreign languages. The Dartmouth requirement in foreign language is stated as "the ability to read with understanding a representative passage in a foreign language," and this is further defined as attainment of a score of 600 or higher on a College Board Achievement Test, or a passing grade in specified courses, normally the fourth-semester course. It is strongly recommended that students continue the language taken in high school, although exceptions are made. All students who have had instruction in the language for which they enroll must either present a score on the appropriate College Board Achievement Test or take a College Board Advanced Placement Test at entrance. On the basis of such a score they are either certified as having met the requirement or assigned to a course consistent with their achievement. Placement ranges from assignment to a course in which a man can complete the requirement in one semester to demotion to the beginning course. The number of years of study of a language in high school is not an infallible index of competence in it.

The College Board Advanced Placement Tests are used as one hour of the final examination in courses above the beginning level, and outstanding students in the beginning course are invited to take them. On the basis of such scores and other evidence the student may complete the requirement, or be given a jump promotion at the end of any semester, or proceed normally through the sequence of courses. The College Board tests are used also as part of the validating examination required of students who seek credit for summer school language courses. Data accumulated over the years by this end-of-course testing, and from studies of scores in relation to course grades, have been used to establish the cutting scores that govern placement. A high proportion of the men who satisfy the requirement by test at entrance elect to continue language study for one or two semesters. About half of the freshmen complete the requirement by the end of two semesters; some who fail courses require more than four semesters.

A similar pattern obtains with respect to the requirement in physical education. All men not medically excused take a series of four physical ability tests devised by the department. Performance on each, and on the total series, is reported in terms of standard scores established over the years on the Dartmouth population. Total score is used to classify men into groups A, B, and C. Men who achieve and maintain an A classification are exempt from classes; men in group B have a choice of courses; men in group C are limited in choice, or may be assigned to special remedial classes. The scores on the specific tests are used diagnostically in this way. The tests are repeated at the end of each semester, and a man may attain a higher group and, hence, exemption or increased freedom at such time. Men who attain B at the end of the third semester have satisfied the requirement, but, failing that, are required to complete four semesters of classes.

EXEMPTION EXAMINATIONS

The establishment of a standing Committee on Proficiency and Placement has given impetus to the program of placement and proficiency exemption in academic subjects. Cognizant of the enormous range of ability and achievement in particular subjects of study present in any entering class, this committee has sought to identify men of outstanding competence; to exempt them from part of the distributive requirement in the areas of their competence; to effect their placement in advanced courses or in honors sections; and in a few cases to grant college credit and resultant advanced standing. The motivation for this work has been the desire to remove exceptionally competent students from the stultifying experience of repeating course work and to place them in a challenging situation where they can progress more rapidly in accordance with their better preparation and greater ability.

During the summer the dean of freshmen examines the secondary school records of all freshmen, selects some 250 men with outstanding records in subjects of study, and writes to them suggesting that they take proficiency tests at entrance. Most of these men, and some additional candidates, do take the tests and some 175 proficiency exemptions are granted. Such exemption gives freedom from part of the distributive requirement, but not college credit nor necessarily advanced course placement; and its significance varies with the subject. For example, a man pursuing a preprofessional program in a science may still be required to take the basic course in physics or chemistry, even though he demonstrated the proficiency required for freedom from part of the distributive requirement in science. On the other hand, he may be relieved of part of the social science requirement by demonstrating proficiency in history. Additional, more difficult tests are used to screen men for advanced course placement in some departments; in others, men are put in honors sections where the pace is faster. In mathematics, for example, no proficiency exemptions are granted, but some seventy-five men selected through scores on the SAT–Mathematical Test and the College Board Advanced Mathematics Test are taught in special sections. Men granted exemption from English 1 are encouraged but not required to elect a special honors course. This is a developing program, which has been stimulated by the work of the School and College Study of Admission with Advanced Standing and by the College Board Advanced Placement Test program.

SERVICES TO THE FACULTY

The Office of Educational Research at Dartmouth operates as a service office available to individual members of the faculty, departments of instruction, committees, and officers of administration. Its services include the typing, reproduction, and assembly of test papers; machine scoring and score reporting; test storage and control; studies of the validity and predictive value of test scores; studies of test questions; and, more generally, consultation and assistance in a variety of research projects. It was created to foster better educational appraisal; it attempts to do so, in part, by facilitating the use of tests and other data-collecting devices and by assisting in the appropriate treatment and use of the data. The problems on which its help is sought run the gamut from admissions to the appraisal of educational experiments.

All use of the office by the faculty is voluntary, with the sole exception that the office calls for copy and reproduces the papers for the formal final examination program. There is a standing Committee on Examinations concerned with the regulation of conditions under which examinations are held; with scheduling, resolution of conflicts, and action on requests to deviate from established regulations; but except in cases of extreme deviation the committee does not control the kind or quality of examinations used. The problem of improving tests and test usage is, therefore, one of moral suasion and assistance, not one of control.

The availability of this service has fostered the development of a large program of objective course examinations, many of them of high quality. The office helps, on request, by providing specimen test forms, by advising on test construction and scoring, and sometimes by critically reviewing the questions. All question-writing is done by the course instructor or course staff. The answer sheets, special pencils, scoring, and all other services are provided without charge against course budgets. Normally, scores are reported within a few hours after receipt of the papers. The test booklets and answer sheets are serially numbered, carefully controlled, stored, and, if the instructor wishes, may be used over a period of years. Such repeated use of good tests is encouraged because it permits comparison of classes from year to year and tends to stabilize grading practice, and because the records of scores made by large populations at the end of a course permit such tests to be used effectively in the course placement or proficiency exemption of entering students.

Objective tests prepared by teachers are used widely both as hour examinations during the semester and as final examinations. Some 40 percent of total course registrations are represented by a machine-scored paper in any final examination period. A system is followed of assigning each machine-scored test an accession number to facilitate filing and control; this number series is now over 1,400. Machine-scored tests are used more commonly in the large beginning courses than in advanced courses, and more commonly in the sciences and social sciences than in the humanities. It is common practice in the social sciences and the humanities to devote one hour of the final examination to an objective test and one hour to the traditional essay test; there is a tendency to use all objective tests in the sciences. In all courses, however, the evidence derived from objective tests constitutes only part of the evidence used in evaluating student achievement and determining course grade.

The careful study of test questions is encouraged both as an aid in test improvement and an aid in instruction. The method of study varies with the case, but always includes a report of the percentage of students who gave the right answer to each question and some index of the question's discriminative power. Questions which prove too easy or too difficult, or which otherwise do not work well, are called to the author's attention for revision or replacement. As an aid in instruction, teachers for some courses request a study of the test questions immediately after scoring. The percentage of students who selected wrong answers to each question is quickly determined and reported to the course staff, who then devote the next class meeting to a discussion of those errors and misunderstandings most prevalent among their students.

At Dartmouth, as elsewhere, the quality of teacher-made tests varies widely, depending on the quality of thinking and the amount of hard work that go into their preparation, and to some extent on the nature of the subject of study and the aptitude of the author for this work. Similarly, understanding of the meaning, limitations, and legitimate uses of the scores from professionally made, published tests varies widely among members of a staff. It is true generally that the preparation of college teachers includes little or no serious study of problems of test construction, test use, interpretation of test results, or of the problems of evaluation in general. This condition, which exists at lower educational levels as well as in the colleges, continues to present a difficult barrier to the optimum use of tests in the educational process.

It is the writer's conviction that every college, no matter how small, ought to have a service office in which the primary responsibility is free-handed assistance to faculty and administration in the collection and processing of educational data. Whether it is called an office of educational research, an office of tests, a research bureau, or an evaluation service, is of little consequence. Precise function may differ with name and the institution, but the fundamental need to be served is clear. The contributions tests can make throughout the many aspects of an educational program have been spelled out in the early chapters of this book. Yet, optimum use of tests and other evaluative devices is held back by two important factors: one is lack of understanding by teachers; the other is the load of time-consuming work involved in test preparation, scoring, and reporting, and the subsequent studies of the results that must be made if the data are to be used effectively. Free-handed assistance with the latter does much to overcome the former, and ultimately to gain for an institution the unquestionable benefits to its educational program that derive from a wise use of tests.

11. The Testing Program of the College of Arts and Sciences of the University of Louisville

J. J. OPPENHEIMER, *Dean of the College*

THE COLLEGE OF ARTS AND SCIENCES IS A PART OF THE UNIVERSITY of Louisville, a municipal university. The college is fifty years old, although the medical unit of the university dates back to 1837. In the last twenty-five years, the enrollment of the college has fluctuated from 800 to a postwar peak of 2,800. Today's enrollment stands at 1,250. The college is coeducational, and, in 1951, the merger of the Municipal College for Negroes with the University of Louisville marked the beginning of integration in all colleges composing the university. Since about 90 percent of its students live in Louisville or Jefferson County, the College of Arts and Sciences is an urban, commuters college.

In 1928, upon the request of the Board of Trustees, Dr. F. J. Kelly, then dean of administration of the University of Minnesota, surveyed the educational needs of the college. Included in the "Kelly Report" was the recommendation that a testing program be established as part of the admissions program for freshmen. In 1929 the American Council Psychological Examination was given for the first time and has been used annually since that date. In 1932 the faculty set up a comprehensive plan of reorganization of the college and included in it a testing program to be used in the admission of all new students, student counseling, the granting of any advanced standing, admission to the senior college, and graduation.

In a real sense the testing program of the college has followed the development of the general nation-wide programs for college testing, for basic policy has been to use only nationally devised tests. As better national tests have been devised, the testing program of this college has been improved. Although those administering the program have felt that such policy is limiting in scope, the college has been without sufficient financial resources to supplement the program with locally designed tests. As a practical matter, however, it is felt that the use of national tests has proved far more adequate than any that like expenditures could have produced locally. In brief, it is believed that for a medium-sized college such as this one, nation-wide tests or programs are of great value.

Upon recommendation of the faculty and the dean of the College of Arts and Sciences, the Testing Service was established in 1932 by the Board of Trustees as a service agency in the office of the dean. The director has the rank of assistant to the dean. Policies governing the administration of the office are determined by regulations established by faculty action, and administration of these policies is carried out under the direction of the dean. Faculty committees, in consultation with the director and the dean, assist in selection of tests and in setting up norms for various purposes.

The Testing Service performs such functions as: scheduling dates for testing, grading tests and recording results, notifying the registrar of the admissibility of new students, notifying students of results of testing and interpreting scores to them, and organizing and distributing monthly reports of test results to faculty, deans, and the registrar. The Testing Service is equipped with an IBM grading machine and scores and reports objective tests for faculty. In addition, the Testing Service is listed as a regional testing agency and regularly administers tests to students from other colleges.

OBJECTIVES OF THE TESTING PROGRAM

The faculty and the dean have always felt that the testing program is an integral part of the educational process of the college. It has been accepted as such on a par with library services, registration, and counseling services. It has been used to provide a means of studying the grading system and the caliber of graduates and for follow-up of graduates. It also represents an attempt to examine by the best means at hand, the academic and intellectual quality of those entering the college, and to ascertain, midway and just before graduation, content achievement in the major areas of learning and in the major subject field. In a broader sense, it provides various kinds of measures of the prevailing curriculum with its elements of teaching and subject matter, as revealed in the learning of students. The testing program is far from a complete measure, and has never been accepted as such; but it has been one kind of measure of the academic accomplishments of both students and faculty. In this same respect, it has served as a control measure of curricular changes.

One of the controversial elements in the 1932 reorganization plan was its program of general education, which at that time was looked upon as far more radical than it would be today. Faculty acceptance of the plan was contingent upon systematic evaluation of the general education courses by testing students in these general areas at the end of their sophomore year. The writer is sure that, if this condition had not been promised, and if students had not achieved standings comparable to the general national average of like colleges, the success of the general education program would have been greatly impaired and the program possibly abandoned. Faculties are conservative when entering into any new educational adventure, and more than "off-the-cuff" faculty opinion is necessary to demonstrate the success of such a venture. Test results furnish substantial bases for sound decision, raising many serious questions in regard to teaching, course content, standards of admission, graduation requirements, and many other academic matters.

Seldom is a subject introduced in our general faculty meetings that some member does not utilize test results as part of his argumentation or suggest further use of this type of evidence. While it would be difficult to verify this point, the writer believes that a testing program, in which nation-wide tests are used, gives the faculty and administration a feeling of security, of self-respect, and of belonging to a group of forward-looking colleges. This should not be interpreted as meaning that the achievements are always satisfying, that is, that they are as much as we should like to see, but rather that they furnish objective guidelines for setting future goals. Without such measures, faculty members would have their own individual ways of determining the intellectual status of the college, and often these estimates are entirely subjective and illusory.

It may seem that undue stress has been placed on the institutional users of tests up to this point, but these are aspects that are ordinarily overlooked. Of course, the prime objective of the testing program is to give the student a more adequate perspective of his abilities and his academic accomplishment. With the aid of faculty counseling, he is able to adjudge his own progress. If the student takes a serious interest in his own education, his standings on the National College Sophomore Tests and the Graduate Record Area Examinations give him some measure of his achievements and his deficiencies, especially in his general education. Also, for many years, the faculty has been interested in the problem of better articulation with the secondary schools and has adopted the policy of accelerating those students who show proficiency in given subjects or areas. Placement of students in appropriate classes has long been a stated objective of this college, and testing has been the major instrument for determining levels of attainment and, in some instances, for granting advanced credit for demonstrated proficiency.

USES OF TESTS

The use made of the testing program will indicate more specifically how the objectives of the program are carried out. All students seeking admission are required to take the freshman battery of tests, which is made up of the following: (1) the American Council Psychological Examination, which yields three scores—quantitative, linquistic, and a total score; (2) the Cooperative English Test, which is comprised of tests in Reading Comprehension, Mechanics of Expression, and Effectiveness of Expression, and provides a total score; and (3) the Cooperative General Culture Test, which is comprised of six subtests covering contemporary social problems, history and social studies, literature, science, fine arts, and mathematics, and provides a total score.

Admission of high school graduates to the college depends on their standings in their graduating classes and their scores on the test battery. Students who make a high enough score are excused from all general education courses with the exception of English Composition.

Since 1934 the college has admitted selected students who have completed three years of senior high school work with selection based on high marks in high school, recommendation of their high school principals, interview, high scores on the freshman test battery, and high scores on the Iowa High School Content Examination. Since 1951 this project has been carried out under a subvention of the Ford Foundation Fund for the Advancement of Education. Mature students who have not had the opportunity to complete their high school education may also be admitted by taking the same battery of tests as the accelerated freshmen and achieving a required standing.

In addition to purposes of admissions, the test data serve other purposes: For example, students who make scores equal to the 65th percentile (national end-of-sophomore-year norms) in the Cooperative test battery, designed annually for use at the sophomore level, may apply for advanced standing credit for general education courses. Students are placed in certain sections of freshman English on the basis of their records in high school English and scores on the Mechanics of English Test. Those who are exceptionally low in this subject are required to take a noncredit course, Fundamentals of English, before entering regular freshman English. Similarly, students who make high scores on local chemistry tests are placed in advanced courses. The same procedure is followed in the modern language courses, and students may be exempt from the language requirement for A.B. degrees by passing language qualifying examinations. Students applying for advanced standing in any field are required to take standardized tests, if available, in addition to departmental examinations. Also, freshman scholarships are awarded on the basis of high test scores, high scholarship standing, and evaluation in interviews. For special guidance purposes, students are given other tests, such as the Kuder Preference Record or the Strong Vocational Interest Blank, or the Wechsler-Bellevue Intelligence Scale.

Since most of the general education courses are concentrated in the first two years, students are required to take sophomore comprehensives at the end of the second year for admission to the senior college. These comprehensives are made up of the Cooperative General Culture Test and the tests in Mechanics of Expression and Effectiveness of Expression. The graduation requirement includes taking the Graduate Record Area Examination, which is comprised of area tests in the social sciences, humanities, and natural sciences, and an advanced test in the major field.

A further illustration of the use of tests is exemplified by a pilot study in the education of elementary teachers. During the past three years the college has been conducting this study under a grant from the Ford Foundation Fund for the Advancement of Education. Students are selected for the program on the basis of their general average in undergraduate colleges and their standing in a series of tests: Graduate Record Area Examination, American Council Psychological Examination, Kuder Preference Record, and the Minnesota Multiphasic Personality Inventory.

NEEDS AND PROBLEMS

This college owes a deep debt of gratitude to the various testing agencies that have contributed so many tests of national scope. As has been indicated, published tests are of particular value to medium-sized colleges that must carry on an effective educational program with limited funds.

Twenty-five years' experience in the use of tests at this college reveals a real need for the improvement of existing tests and the design of new ones, and it is felt that improvement in our testing program might be realized by availability of the following:

1. An up-to-date comprehensive high school test—a measure of high school graduates;
2. A more effective diagnostic reading test for high school graduates;
3. More comprehensive general education tests which should include: (*a*) measurements of attitudes and critical thinking and (*b*) more content of a contemporary nature and less emphasis on the historical aspects of subject matter;
4. A test to appraise English composition on the freshman level;
5. A group test to reveal emotional disturbances of freshmen;

6. Language tests other than German and Romance languages, such as Greek, Russian, and so on;

7. New (or revised) tests for standard college subjects.

It is also felt that the testing services rendered at the college would be improved by:

1. A better understanding on the part of faculty members of the nature of tests given and more effective utilization by faculty members of test results in counseling and in evaluating student growth—also faculty members need to become more expert in test construction in order that they may supplement national tests with those adapted to local objectives;

2. A better understanding on the part of students of the role that testing plays in the furtherance of their own educational objectives;

3. Increased funds for research on the effectiveness of the testing program of this college, as well as for a number of local and special studies; and

4. An increased staff of well-trained personnel to administer testing services.

12. The Testing Program of the Counseling Bureau of the University of Minnesota

RALPH F. BERDIE, *Director of the Student Counseling Bureau, Office of the Dean of Students*

SINCE THEIR INCEPTION THE TESTING PROGRAMS AT THE UNIVERSITY of Minnesota have served the broader counseling purposes of the school. Although few if any large institutions of higher learning can claim to have an all-pervasive educational philosophy, the student personnel point of view has been one of the dominant influences in the development of the educational program at Minnesota.[1] In recognition of the significance of psychological individual differences, and as the result of the effective pioneer work of a few farsighted university administrators and faculty members, the need for adequate counseling has been acknowledged by many staff members and by proportionately even more students.

From its earlier days the Minnesota counseling program has been based upon research, and the needs and characteristics of students have been carefully studied and analyzed.[2] Much of this research has been based on psychological tests, and many of these tests, originally used for research purposes, have been incorporated into the counseling program of the university.

The many testing programs within the university are reviewed periodically to determine how the tests can contribute to the effec-

[1] E. G. Williamson, "Counseling and the Minnesota Point of View," *Educational and Psychological Measurement*, 7:141–55, 1947; E. G. Williamson, *et al.*, *The Student Personnel Point of View* (Washington: American Council on Education, 1949).
[2] E. G. Williamson and J. G. Darley, *Student Personnel Work* (New York: McGraw-Hill Book Co., 1937); C. D. Williams, *These We Teach* (Minneapolis: University of Minnesota Press, 1943).

tive counseling of students. Purposes other than counseling require the extensive use of tests. For instance, admission to some colleges of the university is based in part upon test scores. Students also sometimes are classified into various courses on the basis of test scores. Students who wish to graduate from some of the colleges of the university with honors are required to attain specified scores on certain tests. Many other programs involve the use of special tests, and perhaps all the purposes for which tests are used in other colleges and universities are found also at Minnesota. In every instance, however, consideration is given to the possible use of tests for counseling, even when these tests are being administered for other reasons.

As a result of this counseling emphasis on tests, one must understand the counseling programs at Minnesota if one is to understand the testing programs. A number of centralized university offices provide counseling services to all students. In addition to these centralized offices are other offices in which counselors are concerned only with students from certain divisions of the university. All counseling services and student personnel services are coordinated by the Office of the Dean of Students. The dean of students also is administratively responsible for some of the centralized counseling offices, including the Student Counseling Bureau, the Bureau of Loans and Scholarships, the Discipline Counseling Office, the adviser of foreign students, the Veterans' Counseling Center, the Student Housing Bureau, the Student Activities Bureau, and the Speech and Hearing Clinic. Other departments which provide counseling to all university students include the Mental Hygiene Clinic within the Student Health Service and the Student Employment Bureau.

Although professional counselors in these central counseling offices see thousands of students each year, perhaps the largest number of students are advised and counseled, not in these central programs, but rather in other counseling and advisory programs in the university, particularly faculty advisory programs and residential counseling programs. Central and professional counseling services were developed in the university to supplement faculty advisory programs rather than to substitute for these programs; and much of the time and effort of professional counselors on the campus is devoted to helping faculty advisers, administrators, and others provide better services to students.

The Student Counseling Bureau is responsible for making available to other personnel officers and to faculty members and administrators information about students that will best help the university meet the varied needs of individuals. To obtain this information and to make it available to persons who can use it, the Student Counseling Bureau administers several testing programs. One of these programs extends down into the high schools and involves the administration of over one million tests to pupils in grades nine through twelve in Minnesota schools. Another series of programs has as its purpose the providing of information to college admissions officials to assist them in making decisions regarding individual applicants. Another testing program is more closely related to the orientation program for the new students and involves the administration of ability, interest, and personality tests to entering students for the use of counselors working with these students. A clinical testing service also is maintained for the individual testing of students referred by counselors or other staff members. A number of other special testing programs are administered by the bureau.

In addition to providing information to others in the university who work with students, the Student Counseling Bureau also provides specialized professional counseling services to students; practicum training in counseling to graduate students;[3] in-service training in counseling and testing to college, university, and high school faculties; and consultation to high schools and colleges regarding problems related to testing and counseling.

On the staff of the bureau, in addition to the administrative, supervisory, and clerical workers, are counselors specializing in marriage counseling, educational skills and remedial reading, counseling physically handicapped students, vocational counseling and occupational information, social psychology and group dynamics, and clinical psychology and psychotherapy. Counselors with these specialties do not work only in these restricted fields, but rather, as they counsel all types of students with all types of prob-

[3] R. F. Berdie and Theda Hagenah, "A Training Program in Counseling," *American Psychologist,* 5:140–42, 1950.

lems, they also receive specific referrals of students with problems in their areas, conduct related research, and assist other counselors in broadening and deepening their counseling skills. Not all counselors have specialties as listed above—some work more intensively than others with programs such as residence counseling or orientation programs or with special groups of faculty members or students. Supporting the work of the counselors are psychometrists, statisticians, IBM operators, research assistants and clinical fellows, and a secretarial staff. In 1958, the bureau employed sixteen professional psychologists, four psychometrists, and thirty-one others.

Perhaps the quickest way to comprehend the nature of the university's testing and counseling programs is to follow the progress of a fictitious student through the University. Jerry Smith had his first contact with the university's testing programs when he was in the ninth grade. His school at that time chose to participate in a university testing program and administered to all ninth-grade students the Differential Aptitude Tests and four Cooperative Achievement Tests in mathematics, social studies, natural science, and English. The test supplies were provided to the high school by the university. The tests were administered in the high school, scored by the university, and reported back to the high school. The scores then were recorded on the pupil's cumulative records and used by Jerry's counselors and teachers.

Help was provided to the high school staff by the university so test scores could be used meaningfully. In each school were copies of a manual for the state-wide testing program[4] providing information about the tests. Three times a year the *Student Counseling Bureau Bulletin and Occupational Newsletter* was sent to high schools and university departments to inform them of recent developments in testing and counseling. Research reports were sent to the high schools periodically. Every two years the characteristics of Minnesota high school and college students were analyzed and these reports circulated.[5]

[4] R. F. Berdie, Wilbur L. Layton, and Theda Hagenah, *Using Tests in Counseling: A Manual for the State-Wide Testing Programs of Minnesota* (Minneapolis: Student Counseling Bureau, University of Minnesota, 1953).

[5] R. F. Berdie, W. L. Layton, and E. O. Swanson, "A Follow-up of the Junior Tests Used in the Minnesota State-Wide Testing Program and a Survey of Scholastic Aptitude in Minnesota Colleges" (Mimeographed; Minneapolis: University of Minnesota, 1956).

High school counselors and principals and college counselors are invited to conferences on the university campus to discuss problems of counseling and testing. Occasionally, the bureau helps in conducting conferences elsewhere in the state, and bureau members participate in many professional meetings in Minnesota. Many visits are made by bureau staff members to high schools to discuss testing programs, individual students and their problems, counseling records, and counseling methods. Much of this work has been done in conjunction with the university's College of Education and the State Department of Education.

To return to our student: in the tenth grade the school, again making use of the university's testing program, administered to Jerry and all other tenth-graders the Iowa Tests of Educational Development and the Minnesota Counseling Inventory.[6] Again, these scores were recorded on Jerry's cumulative record and referred to by several of his teachers and by his counselors. In the eleventh grade all pupils were given the Minnesota Scholastic Aptitude Test[7] and the Cooperative English Test as part of a testing program administered by the Student Counseling Bureau of the university and sponsored by the Association of Minnesota Colleges, of which the university is a member.[8] After these tests were scored, all the scores for Minnesota high school juniors were reported to all member colleges of the association and Jerry's scores were reported back to his high school so that his counselors could help him plan during his senior year for his post-high-school activities. During the twelfth grade, the high school administered to Jerry the Strong Vocational Interest Blank and readministered the Iowa Tests of Educational Development and the Minnesota Counseling Inventory. On the basis of changes in test scores, Jerry's counselor was better able to help discuss plans for the future.

Jerry then applied for admission to the College of Science, Literature, and the Arts at the university, and the Admissions Office

---

[6] R. F. Berdie and W. L. Layton, *The Minnesota Counseling Inventory* (New York: Psychological Corporation, 1957).

[7] W. L. Layton, "Construction of a Short Form of the Ohio State University Psychological Examination" (Mimeographed; Minneapolis: University of Minnesota, 1956).

[8] R. F. Berdie, "Guidance between School and College," in *College Admissions*. (Princeton: College Entrance Examination Board, 1956).

referred to his high school percentile rank and his score on the college aptitude test before he was admitted. When he received his admission notification, he was encouraged by his high school counselor to talk with a counselor in the Student Counseling Bureau prior to the beginning of the university year; Jerry came to the bureau and there had three interviews with a counselor. At that time the counselor had Jerry take additional tests, including a reading test, in the bureau testing room. On the basis of this test, and other information, the counselor encouraged Jerry to spend some time developing his reading skills in the Educational Skills Clinic of the bureau. Before the beginning of class, Jerry also attended the two-day orientation and advanced registration program of the university. Here, he took another college aptitude test and the Minnesota Multiphasic Personality Inventory. Other students who had not taken the Strong Vocational Interest Blank in high school were given the test at that time. Students entering other colleges were administered other groups of tests, depending upon the colleges in which they were registering.

All entering freshmen take the interest test. All students, but those in one college, take the Minnesota Multiphasic Personality Inventory; those in the other college take the Minnesota Counseling Inventory. Students in the College of Science, Literature, and the Arts take an additional college aptitude test. In the Institute of Technology they take an algebra test and, sometimes, the Layton Engineering Aptitude Test. General College students are given the General Aptitude Test Battery of the U. S. Office of Employment. Education students take the Minnesota Teacher Attitude Inventory and the Cooperative Reading Comprehension Test. Scores on all these tests are reported to college offices and are available to faculty advisers.

During his first two years in the Arts College, Jerry completed some work in the Educational Skills Clinic and two or three times spoke with the counselor he had seen prior to the beginning of school. Each quarter he also met with his college adviser, who helped him plan his academic program and discussed other matters with him.

At the completion of his sophomore year, Jerry was considering majoring in one of the departments that required all its students to take the Cooperative General Culture Test; and, consequently, Jerry took this test and his scores were reported to the college office and used there by the adviser who discussed with Jerry senior college alternatives.

Let us assume now that Jerry had decided he would study medicine. At the time he applied for admission to the Medical School, he was informed that he would have to take two groups of tests. The national tests required by most medical colleges and administered by the Educational Testing Service are given by the Student Counseling Bureau, and another group of tests required by the University of Minnesota Medical School are also administered by the bureau. These test scores all were made available to the Medical School Admissions Committee and also to Jerry's counselor, who was in a position to discuss with him their counseling implications.

When Jerry was tested in the eleventh grade, a permanent university record card was initiated and his eleventh-grade test scores were recorded on this card. When he was given the interest test in the twelfth grade, this fact was noted on his card and a copy of his interest profile was placed in the files. From that time, every time Jerry took a test in the university, his scores were entered on the basic record card. The tests taken at the request of Student Counseling Bureau counselors were included in his counseling folder and kept in an adjacent file.

Jerry's faculty adviser had made available to him by the college office the eleventh-grade test scores and the scores of tests taken during the orientation program. These scores are reported as a matter of routine to the college offices by the Student Counseling Bureau. At any time that Jerry's adviser wanted additional test information from the Student Counseling Bureau, this was available by calling the Faculty-Student Contact Desk, the division of the bureau that coordinates all available information concerning counseling contacts and test scores. When Jerry's adviser called the Contact Desk for additional information, he would be given not only whatever test scores were available, but also the names of any other counselors on the campus who had seen Jerry. In this instance, he would be told that a bureau counselor also had talked with Jerry and, in turn, the bureau counselor would be notified of the call to the desk from Jerry's adviser.

Not every student goes through this rather intensive testing. For instance, many high schools do not use all of these tests. Many university students do not see a bureau counselor and consequently do not take those tests. Students entering certain colleges within the university are not required to take admissions tests and, consequently, for many students rather meager test information is available. For practically all university students, however, some information is available concerning general academic aptitude and, for an increasing number, information is available concerning measured vocational interests and measured personality characteristics. •

We should repeat that test scores are of little value unless people are trained and motivated to use them properly. Consequently, much of the professional counselors' time is devoted to working with individual university staff members to assist them in understanding the meaning of test scores. The bureau organizes and conducts systematic programs that bring together groups of staff members to present them with an opportunity to discuss testing problems. For instance, during one year a series of several meetings was held to which all faculty members and personnel workers were invited to discuss vocational interest measurement. During another year a similar series of meetings was devoted to the discussion of personality tests and during still another year, the discussion centered around the measurement of academic aptitude. The *Student Counseling Bureau Newsletter* is distributed to approximately five hundred university staff members and reports current information on the use of tests. Professional counselors also work closely with resident counselors and much time is spent when resident counselors consult with bureau counselors concerning individual cases and counseling problems.

A testing program of this nature can be maintained at a high level only if the research upon which it is based also thrives. New tests are constantly being developed. During recent years a new personality test, the Minnesota Counseling Inventory; a new academic aptitude test, the Minnesota Scholastic Aptitude Test; and a new engineering aptitude test, the Layton Engineering Aptitude Test, have been standardized. Prediction studies are conducted periodically to provide to counselors and other staff members current information concerning the predictive power of tests.[9] An analysis recently has been completed showing the changes or lack of changes in the characteristics of college students during the past twenty-five years. Another series of experiments has been completed exploring the use of tests and related information in group counseling situations.[10]

In summary, the primary purpose of the testing programs at the University of Minnesota is to provide to students, their instructors, and their counselors information that will best help in the solution of educational, vocational, and personal problems. University testing also serves many other purposes, but only this primary purpose provides justification for the extensive program here described.

[9] R. F. Berdie and N. A. Sutter, "Predicting Success of Engineering Students," *Journal of Educational Psychology,* 14:184–90, 1950; R. F. Berdie and W. L. Layton, "Predicting Success in Law School," *Journal of Applied Psychology,* 4:257–60, 1952; W. L. Layton, "Predicting Success of Students in Veterinary Medicine," *Journal of Applied Psychology,* 36:312–15, 1952; W. L. Layton, and E. O. Swanson, "A Follow-up of Minnesota State-Wide Program Test Results in the Institute of Technology" (Mimeographed; Minneapolis: University of Minnesota, 1957).

[10] D. P. Hoyt, "An Evaluation of Group and Individual Programs in Vocational Guidance," *Journal of Applied Psychology,* 39:26–30, 1955.

13. The Testing Program of Pasadena City College

W. B. LANGSDORF, *President*
FLORENCE BRUBAKER, *Dean of Student Personnel*

PASADENA CITY COLLEGE IS A TWO-YEAR PUBLIC JUNIOR COLLEGE with an enrollment of 4,600 students in its day program. The student body includes students who wish to parallel the first two years of a four-year college or university program, students who wish to take one or two years of specialized vocational training, and students who wish to make up high school grade or subject deficiencies. Last year's student body represented 849 high schools, 48 states, and 64 foreign countries.

Under California law public junior colleges must accept all high school graduates and all others over the age of eighteen whom the college believes may profit from the education offered. The student body is, therefore, unselected and represents a wide range of abilities and interests. At one end of the scale in scholastic ability are the one hundred to one hundred and fifty students in each class who have an A— or better high school grade average. At the other end are a few students with IQ's as low as 80 or 90. A major function of the public junior college is guidance and placement of students in curricula for which they are qualified. Pasadena City College, while not selective in admissions, is selective in admission to specific curricula and courses, primarily on the basis of high school achievement or achievement in junior college.

The basic testing program in such a college, therefore, is not a selective admissions device, but rather an attempt to provide a uniform basis for evaluating the achievements and interests of its students, as well as to obtain an objective appraisal of individual scholastic aptitude and ability. It supplements scholastic achievement in class placement.

The present basic testing program is a minimum one, all freshmen taking the American Council Psychological Examination[1] the fourth week of the semester in connection with a required Basic Communication class. The Cooperative English Test, Mechanics of Expression, is given to all students in freshman English classes during the first week of the semester and is used, together with instructor evaluations, to verify placement in regular or remedial classes. All freshmen also are given a speech, a library, and a listening test (developed by members of the faculty) in their Basic Communication classes.

Specialized individual testing (on interest, aptitude, ability, projective personality) is available through the services of a psychologist assisted by a psychometrist. Such testing may be requested by students, counselors, the health center, or members of the faculty and administration, all requests being channeled through the dean of student personnel. Through individual counselor interviews, students plot profile charts of their scores on the ACE Psycological Examination and Cooperative English Tests. Results of specialized tests are released to appropriate staff personnel and interpreted to students by the psychologist. Faculty members are asked to consult the student's counselor or the psychologist for personal data regarding students.

There is a growing tendency to use achievement tests as placement tools in specific areas of science and mathematics. Such tests are administered by the psychometrist prior to registration. The ACE Psychological Examination and Cooperative English Tests probably should, and soon may, be given prior to registration. The Lado English Language Test for Foreign Students[2] has been found to be most helpful in the counseling of foreign students. This also will be administered by the psychometrist prior to registration.

The present year is a transition period for testing practices at Pasadena City College. In addition to the psychologist and nine full-time counselors who have long served the student body, a full-time psychometrist has just been added to the staff. It is planned that the basic testing program, as well as many of the aptitude and personality tests, will be administered by him, freeing more of the time of the psychologist for test interpretation, psychological counseling, and casework. General supervision of the stu-

---

[1] With the withdrawal recently of this examination, Pasadena is now considering several other tests as possible replacements.

[2] Published by George Wahr Publishing Co., 316 South State St., Ann Arbor, Mich.

dent testing services is assigned to the dean of student personnel. The psychometrist organizes and administers the group testing program for entering students in cooperation with the dean of student personnel, the psychologist, and the coordinator of Basic Communication (an orientation program required of freshmen); administers and scores placement tests in specialized areas as requested; administers individual interest, ability, and aptitude tests as requested by administrators, psychologist, counselors, and teachers; and administers specialized tests of the General Aptitude Test Battery of the U. S. Office of Employment or proficiency tests as requested by the Placement Office.

The psychologist administers tests such as the Wechsler Adult Intelligence Scale, the Strong Vocational Interest Blank, Diagnostic Reading Tests, Leiter Adult Intelligence Scale,[3] and a variety of aptitude and projective personality tests.

Test data are filed in the student's folder in the office of his counselor, or, in some instances, kept in the confidential file of the psychologist. Upon request, such data are interpreted to faculty by the student's counselor. They are used by the counselor in advising students with special regard to their educational and vocational planning. Some of the more general test data, such as ACE Psychological Examination, the Cooperative English Test, and the listening and speech tests, are studied by the student in his Basic Communication class.

Among the problems facing junior colleges relative to measurement are the following:

1. What constitutes a minimum, yet adequate, testing program?
2. How can we detect, through a minimum group testing program, those students with reading or other handicaps whose potential (or true) ability is not shown on available group tests with high verbal loading?
3. Do the wide discrepancies often found between the scores made on individual tests, such as the Wechsler Adult Intelligence Scale and available group tests, indicate that a new type of group test is needed in situations where students present widely variant personal and educational backgrounds?
4. How can we provide adequate vocational interest testing (such as the Strong Vocational Interest Blank) at a feasible cost?

[3] Published by C. H. Stoelting Co., 424 North Homan Ave., Chicago 24, Ill.

14. The Testing Program of San Francisco State College[1]

ALAN W. JOHNSON, *Associate Dean of Students*
F. GRANT MARSH, *Coordinator of Testing*
JOSEPH AXELROD, *Curriculum Evaluator*

SAN FRANCISCO STATE COLLEGE IS ONE OF TEN INSTITUTIONS MAKING up the California state college system. This system is supported by public funds and is, of course, subject to legal control of the State Board of Education and the laws of California.

The primary educational functions of the state colleges are to provide: (1) liberal education, with an emphasis on general education in the lower division; (2) teacher education, providing preservice and in-service education of teachers for the public schools; (3) occupational training through curricula requiring four or five years of college training; and (4) preprofessional education with training leading to graduate work in the major professions and research fields.

San Francisco State College has been a leader in the development of a specially designed general education program required of all students. The major fields of study offered by the eight academic divisions of the college provide a wide variety of liberal education and occupational training. The college is authorized to award bachelor's degrees in the arts, education, science, and vocational education, the master of arts degree, and a large variety of teaching credentials.

The college is located on a ninety-three-acre campus in San Francisco and draws most of its student population from the San

[1] Alan W. Johnson and F. Grant Marsh, staff members of the Office of the Dean of Students, are responsible for the section of this paper dealing with admissions and credential tests; Joseph Axelrod, a staff member of the Office of the Dean of Instruction, is responsible for the section dealing with the use of tests and other evaluation instruments in the instructional program.

Francisco Bay Area. In the fall 1957 semester there were enrolled on campus approximately 6,100 full-time students and 3,700 part-time students; in addition, 3,700 students are enrolled in off-campus extension courses. New regular students enter in almost equally divided numbers as freshmen or as transfer students from junior colleges or from other four-year institutions.

ADMISSIONS AND CREDENTIAL TESTING

Admission standards at San Francisco State College are specified in the California Administrative Code, which provides uniform admissions regulations for all California state colleges. These regulations are, of course, complex, but a summary of them will be useful for those involved in admissions testing at other institutions.

Policies concerning admission to the college

A high school graduate is admitted if he has completed the equivalent of seven Carnegie units of course work in subjects other than physical education and military science, with grades of A or B on a five-point scale during the last three years in high school. If the high school graduate is able to present only the equivalent of five Carnegie units instead of seven, he may still gain admission if he attains at minimum the 20th percentile on the national college freshman norms of a standard college aptitude test.

Veterans and applicants over twenty-one years of age who are not high school graduates but whose scores on the college entrance examinations indicate ability to do satisfactory college work may be granted admission. An applicant who has earned credit in other colleges and universities may be admitted if he meets standards as follows: (1) he must have a grade-point average of at least 2.0 (grade C on a five-point scale) on the total program attempted, or (2) he may receive special consideration if he attains the 20th percentile on the national norms of a standard college aptitude test.

A student may be admitted to graduate standing if he holds a bachelor's degree from an accredited institution. For admission to candidacy for the master's degree program, he must have a B average in all postbaccalaureate work, must have taken the Graduate Record Area Examination, and must give evidence of a foundation in his field sufficient to indicate probable success in the program.

Testing of applicants for admission to the college

All applicants for admission as regular students, except graduates of four-year accredited colleges and universities and applicants from foreign lands, are required to take entrance examinations prior to final action on their applications. Applicants are tested in large groups on specific dates which are scheduled throughout the year.

The entrance battery includes: (1) the School and College Ability Tests (the American Council Psychological Examination was used prior to 1956–57) and (2) the Cooperative English Tests, Mechanics of Expression and Reading Comprehension. These tests were selected because of their ease of administration to large groups and because they seemed to be the best available to furnish information about the applicants' ability to pursue college work and to detect any deficiencies in their ability to handle the English language.

Occasionally the Admissions Office may request the coordinator of testing to retest an applicant. There are various reasons for such requests, a common one arising when an applicant meets all the qualifications for admission but performs poorly on the entrance examinations. It may be that he has been away from school or college for some time or that his Carnegie units were earned in courses other than in academic subjects (for example, music, art, shop, typing, and so on). Usually the Ohio State Psychological Test, the Wechsler-Bellevue Intelligence Scale, the Henmon-Nelson Tests of Mental Ability (college), and the ACE Psychological Examination are used for retesting. The selection of the test is determined by the nature of the case and the time available for administering it.

All freshman students are required to take a sequence of two three-unit courses in Basic Communication to develop skill in reading, writing, speaking, and listening. Undergraduate transfer students who have not completed six units in English composition are required to take three or six units in Basic Communication. Remedial laboratories in reading and writing are available to help students improve reading and study techniques and to improve the effectiveness of their writing. Scores on the Cooperative English Tests in Reading Comprehension and Mechanics of Expression are used by the Testing Office in determining which students should enroll in these laboratories, in addition to regular enrollment in the required courses in Basic Communication. Tentatively a cutting scaled score of 55 on these tests has been established. These tests have been in use only two years, and no studies have been completed on their effectiveness, although two are now in process. In addition to the reading and writing tests, a short test in speech performance is given to new students prior to registration for the purpose of discovering which among them should be referred to a remedial speech laboratory.

The results of all tests in the entrance battery are available for the use of administrative staff and faculty.

Prior to 1956–57, the ACE Psychological Examination was included in the entrance battery. No studies were made of its effectiveness in predicting success. The School and College Ability Tests (SCAT) have been in use for one year. With the installation of IBM equipment this year, it is hoped that a study of the effectiveness of SCAT can be made.

Admission to teacher education programs and candidacy for teaching credentials

Candidates for admission to teacher education curricula are judged on the following bases: intelligence, scholarship, satisfactory completion of at least two years of college level work, professional aptitude, physical fitness, speech and language usage, personality and character, and diversity of interests. Concerning the first factor in the foregoing list, California State law reads: "Any candidate who falls below the 25th percentile on the national college norms of a generally recognized college aptitude test must demonstrate compensating strength in other qualities." Results on SCAT or on the ACE Psychological Examination (prior to fall 1956) taken at the time of entrance, are furnished to the Education Division for use in weighing candidates on the intelligence factor. Under the law, the factors of professional aptitude and personality and character are to be evaluated by tests, observations, and interviews, and determination of the results are to be made by committee action. Use of tests to assess professional aptitude, personality, and character of credential candidates has been very limited.

No person may be employed as teacher or administrator in a California public school unless he holds a credential issued by the State Board of Education. Requirements for the credential are established by the board, and provide, among other things, that credential candidates shall demonstrate proficiency not only in oral and written language but in several other areas as well. San Francisco State College has prescribed a battery of competency tests which students must pass; if they fail to do so, they must successfully complete a course which covers the subject matter and skills measured by the test. Students are advised to take the competency tests at the close of their sophomore year or as soon thereafter as possible, so that deficiencies may be corrected before they enter their professional programs. Students may not enroll in student teaching courses until all the required competencies have been demonstrated and candidacy for the credential has been granted.

The competency tests administered to elementary credential candidates are outlined below:

1. Locally constructed tests covering the fields of art, geography, music, nature study, physical education, speech, and written English skills.
2. Published tests:
   a) Until the fall of 1957 the Iowa Every-Pupil Test of Basic Arithmetic Skills, advanced battery, Forms L, M, and N were employed. National norms were used, and the ninth-grade equivalent was required.
      Beginning in the fall of 1957 the Q score on SCAT has been substituted for the Iowa Every-Pupil Test in arithmetic.
   b) Cooperative English Test, Reading Comprehension, Forms T and Z; local norms are used for the different college years; candidates must attain the 40th percentile for passing.

The competency tests administered to secondary credential candidates are as follows:

1. Locally constructed tests covering the fields of speech and written English skills.
2. Published tests:
   a) Cooperative English Test, Reading Comprehension, Forms T and Z; local norms are used for the different college years; candidates must attain the 40th percentile for passing.
   b) Cooperative Test of General Culture; three of the five parts must be completed at a satisfactory level.

Admission to other curricula

Systematic use of admissions test results in determining admission of candidates to curricula other than teacher education is carried on in only one major field of work. This is the clinical science curriculum for the training of laboratory technicians. Applicants for this course of study must rank above the 40th percentile on national norms on the ACE Psychological Examination or on SCAT. The results on this and other tests are, however, used extensively for educational and vocational counseling and by major advisers working with their advisees.

THE USE OF TESTS IN THE INSTRUCTIONAL PROGRAM

In addition to the wide use of tests at San Francisco State College in its entrance battery for freshmen and transfer students seeking admission, in the competency testing of candidates for the credential program, and in the admission of candidates to the graduate curricula, the college has, of course, found testing indispensable for its instructional program. The use of tests has been important not only in serving as a main means of evaluating student progress and achievement for the purpose of assigning course grades,[2] but it has also been important, especially during the last half-dozen years, in the systematic attempts by our instructors and course staffs to judge the effectiveness of their instruction.

The role of a central office in self-appraisal projects by instructional staff

An Office of Curriculum Evaluation was set up in 1951. Its primary purpose was to encourage and help initiate self-appraisal programs in every curricular area ready for such scrutiny, and to aid individual instructors, in whatever ways it could, in their efforts to improve the effectiveness of their own courses. The office is staffed by a curriculum evaluator and his secretary. Additional

[2] In a survey carried on about three years ago among our faculty who teach general education courses (numbering over one hundred), it was discovered that for 36 percent of the faculty, test scores had an 85 percent, *or greater,* weight in determining the course grade and that, for well over half the faculty, test scores had a 55 percent, *or greater,* weight in determining the course grade. Only 11 percent of the faculty indicated the weight given to test scores in determining the course grade was less than 15 percent.

aid is obtainable when needed, both in the way of faculty advice and help and of clerical assistance. During the first several years of the existence of the office, an all-college Advisory Committee on Evaluation met monthly with the evaluator, but once the office achieved stability in its functioning and once its services to faculty members became well known, such a faculty committee no longer proved necessary.

It is important to realize that, at San Francisco State College, the evaluator does not function as an administrative officer but that he and his office are wholly designed to be of service to the several divisions of the college and their individual faculty members. He plays no part in such matters as staffing and scheduling of courses and promotions. He is a member of the staff of the Office of the Dean of Instruction, but, while he may help a staff or instructor prepare or select appropriate tests for a project in self-appraisal or may help in the design of the project and in the collection and interpretation of data, he does not submit to the dean of instruction the findings of projects he helps individual instructors carry out. This type of relationship to the faculty members whom he serves and to the dean under whose general supervision he works is imperative if instructors are to continue to make use of the evaluator's services for the purpose of discovering their weaknesses and strengths as teachers.

In other aspects of his work, the evaluator may play a more official role. For example, suppose one of the teaching staffs brings a proposal for a change in some aspect of the instructional program to the committee for consideration, and the committee decides it needs more data. It may ask the curriculum evaluator to procure the data and report directly to the committee, or it may ask the course staff to consult with the evaluator on the best way of proceeding to collect the data and later to report back to the committee when the data are compiled.

From the preceding description, some of the philosophic principles can be inferred upon which the work of the Office of Curriculum Evaluation is built. Its ultimate goal is neither the construction or use of tests, nor the compilation of data, nor even the analysis of strengths and weaknesses in a present or proposed course or curriculum; these are all means toward its ultimate goal, which is the improvement of instruction.[3]

Faculty self-appraisal projects involving tests of student achievement

Many of the evaluation projects have, of course, begun with the collection of data on student achievement. We must admit that the problem of discovering or constructing achievement tests adequate for our purposes has remained a major problem. Where the skill or the body of knowledge over which mastery is being tested is, in our view, adequately measured in a published test, it is obviously a great advantage to us to purchase and use it. If we were to attempt to construct and refine our own instrument, we would probably have a less reliable and, in the end, much more expensive one. But with the exception of the tests mentioned in succeeding paragraphs, published tests have not generally suited our purposes, especially where we have needed them most—namely, in the four broad areas of our general education goals.

Our staffs are, however, most interested in the publication of folios of large numbers of test items (rather than individual tests) from among which they may select the exercises which, in their judgment, test for the goals held significant by the staff itself. In a subsequent section dealing with our television experiment in general education courses, mention will be made of the use to which such a folio in the field of the natural sciences (published by the Educational Testing Service) has already been put.

Some of the instruments which have been used to collect data on student achievement for analysis in various evaluation projects are as follows: The Health Inventories (Cooperative Test Division of the Educational Testing Service); the English Structure Test (developed at the University of Michigan and used in projects with our overseas students); the Iowa Silent Reading Test; the University of California Subject A Examination; the Diagnostic Reading Tests (Educational Records Bureau). A project appraising improvement in logical reasoning used a locally developed instru-

[3] For a full statement of the philosophy of evaluation too briefly summarized here, see Joseph Axelrod, "Evaluation versus Mumblety-Peg: How To Appraise a Program in Curriculum Evaluation," *Educational Record*, 35:305–12, October 1954.

ment adapted from several of the latest forms of the Progressive Education Association instruments used in the Eight-Year Study.[4] A project attempting to measure growth in critical thinking used a locally constructed essay test, in which a special scoring procedure was worked out involving anonymity of both student and year (that is, whether pre- or post-test) and two independent readers for each essay booklet. In one project measuring the effectiveness of the general education two-semester required course in psychology, the entire department participated in the construction of an instrument for pre- and post-test purposes.[5] In addition to the foregoing, student achievement tests used in the television experiment will be listed in a later section.

Evaluation projects involving instruments other than achievement tests

The evaluation projects have not always, of course, called for the use of achievement tests. A number of the projects have sought to collect and analyze faculty opinion or student opinion on certain issues or courses. Aside from the questionnaire type of instrument, a number of projects have used sociometric tests or rating scales on which faculty judgments are recorded. Two projects, proceeding on the assumption that effectiveness of instruction in a multiple-section course was closely allied with the functioning of the course staff as a group working cooperatively, studied course staffs by means of such tests and scales. All of these instruments were locally constructed, although a number were actually local adaptations of instruments developed elsewhere.[6]

[4] These were adapted to our needs by the Office of Curriculum Evaluation with the help of Dr. Hilda Taba, who was at that time a member of the college-wide Advisory Committee on Evaluation.

[5] All these projects are described in detail in mimeographed "Evaluation Reports," which were issued to the faculty. Copies are available on loan to interested readers. Summaries of all these are given in another mimeographed document, "A Report on Evaluation in General Education at San Francisco State College: Summaries of Twenty-Seven Evaluation Reports Submitted to the Committee on General Education," also available on loan from the college. Some of the projects and some of the instruments used in them (with illustrations) are described by Joseph Axelrod, "The Evaluation of the General Education Program at San Francisco State College," in Paul L. Dressel (ed.), *Evaluation in General Education Programs* (Dubuque, Ia.: Wm. C. Brown Co., 1954).

[6] These are partly reproduced in Paul L. Dressel and Lewis B. Mayhew, *General Education: Explorations in Evaluation* (Washington: American Council on Education, 1954).

A number of the projects used more than single tests. One ambitious study, for example, evaluating the effectiveness of our general education course in Home and Family Living, used the Bell Adjustment Inventory (student form); the Mooney Problem Check List (college form); a locally constructed subject-matter test; a locally constructed projective test (incomplete sentence type); a student rating scale consisting of questions about the course and the instructor; recorded counseling interviews; and a course evaluation form.[7]

Tests used in the television experiment in general education courses

San Francisco State College is now carrying on experimentation, under a grant from the Fund for the Advancement of Education, to compare instruction by television with instruction through traditional media. In the first phase of the project (1956–57), the following instruments were used in addition to tests of subject matter: the Edwards Personal Preference Schedule; Personal Inventory (Self-Insight Scale), which is partly standardized;[8] Bills' Index of Adjustment of Values, which is standardized but not available in published form;[9] the California Auding Test, Form F, revised, 1952, by Brown and Caffrey (published by the Council on Auding Research, Redwood City, California); and a locally devised sociometric test. Additional data on the students included test scores on the ACE Psychological Examinations and SCAT as well as information not obtained through tests.

In the second phase of the television experiment, currently under way, similar instruments are being employed. One of the achievement tests, the Hills Economics Test, is standardized, but

---

[7] The research for this evaluation project was done as part of a doctoral dissertation by Duncan V. Gillies, "Three Methods of Teaching a College Course in Home and Family Living in a General Education Program" (Unpublished, Stanford University, 1952).

Two other doctoral dissertations were, in fact, evaluation studies of aspects of the general education program: Florence C. Haimes, "Physical Sciences in the General Education Program of a State College," and Arthur J. Hall, "An Evaluation of a College Course in Occupational Development" (both Stanford University; 1952 and 1949 respectively).

[8] Personal Inventory (Self-Insight Scale) appeared in the *Journal of Social Psychology*, 219–36, November 1948.

[9] Bills' Index of Adjustment of Values appeared in the *Journal of Consulting Psychology*, 257–61, 1951.

the others are locally constructed. One of these, covering the field of natural sciences, consists of items selected from a published test folio.[10] In addition, the project is using: the Watson-Glaser Critical Thinking Appraisal; Individual Inventory (Self-Insight), developed and partly standardized by L. Grose, Syracuse University; the Edwards Personal Preference Schedule; Attitude Scales, developed at Miami University, Oxford, Ohio; a Degree of Interest Scale, developed at the Pennsylvania State University; and sociometric tests locally devised.[11]

Tests used by instructors for assigning course grades

About three years ago, the Curriculum Evaluation Office carried on a survey of faculty opinion about the tests they were using in their courses. A questionnaire was used, which was answered anonymously. The survey was carried on among the faculty teaching one or more sections of a general education course; this involved more than a third of the total faculty.

When the faculty members were asked whether they felt their examinations were successfully measuring the degree to which students were attaining the basic purposes of their courses, only 37 percent answered "Yes" and an additional 19 percent answered "Yes, with reservations." It is interesting that this percentage was *smaller* than that given in a similar survey made a year and a half before, and that in the interim attempts had been made to achieve greater awareness among faculty members of the problems in test construction for general education courses.

Another question asked: "If an informal faculty seminar were organized (with membership completely voluntary) to study ways of improving testing procedures and appraisal of student achieve-

[10] Paul L. Dressel and Clarence H. Nelson, *Questions and Problems in Science: Test Item Folio No. 1* (Princeton, N.J.: Educational Testing Service, 1957).

[11] A published report on this first phase of the project appeared in 1958: Robert E. Dreher and Walcott H. Beatty, *An Experimental Study of College Instruction Using Broadcast Television,* Project No. 1, San Francisco State College, sponsored by the Fund for the Advancement of Education (San Francisco, Calif.: The College, April 1958). Additional information about these experiments may be had from the following San Francisco State College faculty members: Robert E. Dreher and Walcott Beatty, who were, respectively, project director and evaluator for 1956-57; Albert R. Lepore and Jack D. Wilson, who are, respectively, project director and evaluator currently.

ment in your area, do you think it would be worth your while to attend some or all of its sessions?" Over two-thirds of the faculty answered "Yes." Unfortunately, it was impossible to carry out plans for a full-fledged seminar, but the curriculum evaluator met with several of the course staffs to discuss the construction of tests in their area, and meetings between faculty members and the evaluator, individually or in very small groups, to discuss such problems, are part of the regular routine of the Evaluation Office. The evaluator frequently instructs faculty members in the mechanics of converting a hand-scored objective test to a machine-scored one and in the rewording of items. It is inevitable and desirable that more than merely mechanical features be treated.

Several of the questions in the faculty survey sought to discover from instructors whether students could average C or better on their examinations through memorization alone. Well over a third of the faculty responded that this appeared to them to be true.

Two additional pieces of data gathered by the questionnaire concerned a problem that is frequently encountered in the construction of teacher-made objective tests and in the grading of essay tests. Instructor-made tests of the objective type often use ambiguous wording so that the better students are often penalized. The evaluator, in working on this problem with faculty members discovered, as he expected to, that this feature was substantially improved after attempts were made to persuade instructors to add an *indispensable* step in the process of test construction: to ask one or two colleagues to run through the items in their draft form. It was gratifying therefore to discover, in the faculty survey, that *almost half* of the instructors who used tests of the objective type (40 percent indicated that they used the essay type *only*) said they did generally carry on this practice before the typing of their final test copy.

On the essay type of test, the equivalent problem is that of reliability in grading. And the equivalent solution is for instructors to ask a colleague to grade some or all of the papers independently (in accordance with the original instructor's criteria for judging the essays) and to analyze the extent and bases of disagreements in the grades assigned. Here, too, attempts were made, always on the informal level, to demonstrate that this was a worth-while practice. In the survey, about one-third of the faculty members who used essay tests (26 percent indicated they used the objective type of test *only*) said they had tried using this method. A number who said they had not indicated, however, in their written comments that they used some other method of ensuring minimum reliability in the grading of essay tests.[12]

Some institutions have attempted to solve a number of the problems discussed here by setting up an examiner's office, staffed by testing experts who are given the responsibility of constructing adequate examinations and administering them to students. Such an office is particularly appropriate for programs in which many of the courses are multiple-section courses, as they are in the general education program at San Francisco State College. One of the evaluation reports, in the process of analyzing the problem of achieving common grading standards in a multiple-section course with a fairly large staff, presents a review of the arguments for and against the centralized examination system as a solution to problems in testing and grading.[13] The college, however, has never seriously considered the possibility of setting up a central examining agency as the primary means of certifying that students have fulfilled the college requirements in general education. It is nevertheless true that from time to time some of the course staffs have considered the possibility of constructing and using common tests in their multiple-section course.

We do not have recent data on this matter, but the earlier of the two faculty surveys referred to above gives us faculty opinion and practice on this question in 1952. At that time, 60 percent of the faculty teaching in the general education program said that they had used test exercises in their exams which were prepared for common use by staff members, even though this was not a regular practice. An attempt, too, was made to discover how many of the faculty believed that a certain amount of common testing materials

[12] The mimeographed report of this survey, Evaluation Report No. 6: "Faculty Opinion on Testing Problems in the General Education Courses" is available on loan from the college.

[13] Evaluation Report No. 7: "The Problem of Course Grades and Grading Standards in General Education Courses" (mimeographed); available on loan from the college.

ought to be used by every instructor teaching different sections of their course. Almost 80 percent of the faculty said that they shared this belief. The faculty was further asked its opinion on the specific amount that should be common to all instructors in the course. Almost 40 percent said they could not answer the question; but of those who had an opinion, three-fourths said they believed *half or more* of the examinations in their general education courses should consist of *common* test exercises.

Subsequently, a number of the general education course staffs did work out common test exercises, but their use has been completely voluntary, and the degree to which the score on any test determines the student's course grade remains entirely a decision of the individual instructor.

One of the objects in setting up a separate examiner's office is to relieve instructors of the task of constructing their own tests and giving their own grades; and one of the arguments in favor of this policy is that testing and appraising student achievement is a task which, to be effectively performed, requires an amount of time and the possession of skills which, on the whole, college instructors are unwilling to give and do not possess. The policy at San Francisco State is, however, not to relieve the instructor of these tasks, but rather to take steps which will enable him to perform the appraisal tasks more adequately than most college instructors are apparently able to do at the present time.[14]

In pursuing this policy, not only the Office of Curriculum Evaluation and the Testing Office but also a large number of the administrative officers of the college have given encouragement and service.

[14] Some of our staff members, it must be said, have become especially interested in testing problems. Outside the field of psychology, whose staff members have been specially trained in the techniques, two efforts are worth noting here. One faculty member has been interested in developing instruments that are machine-scored and also open-book; another has developed exercises for his own courses using the Objective Test of Essay Answers technique expounded by Leo Nedelsky, "Evaluation of Essays by Objective Tests," *Journal of General Education*, 209–20, April 1953.

Bibliography

American Association of Collegiate Registrars and Admissions Officers, Committee on Machine Equipment. *Machine Equipment for Efficient Office Operation.* The Association, 1954.

American Council on Education. *Cooperation in General Education: A Final Report of the Executive Committee on Cooperative Study in General Education.* Washington: The Council, 1947.

American Educational Research Association. "Growth, Development and Learning," *Review of Educational Research,* 25:473 ff., December 1955.

Bloom, Benjamin S., and Krathwohl, D. R. *Taxonomy of Educational Objectives.* New York: Longmans, Green & Co., 1956.

Brouwer, Paul A. *Student Personnel Services in General Education.* Washington: American Council on Education, 1949.

Buros, Oscar K. (ed.). *Mental Measurement Yearbooks.* Highland Park, N.J.: Gryphon Press. Latest edition, 1953.

Chatham College, Office of Evaluation Services. *Bulletins.* Pittsburgh, Pa.: The College.

College Board Review. Princeton, N.J.: College Entrance Examination Board.

College Entrance Examination Board. *Advanced Placement Program.* Princeton, N.J.: The Board, 1957.

College Entrance Examination Board. *College Admissions 1, 2, 3, 4.* Princeton, N.J.: The Board.

Cornell, Francis G. "Sample Surveys in Education," *Review of Educational Research,* 24:359, December 1954.

Cronbach, Lee J. *Essentials of Psychological Testing.* New York: Harper & Bros., 1949.

Davis, Allison. *Social-Class Influences Upon Learning.* Cambridge, Mass.: Harvard University Press, 1948.

Dressel, Paul L. "Evaluation Procedures for General Education Objectives," *Educational Record,* 31:97–122, April 1950.

Dressel, Paul L., and Mayhew, Lewis B. *General Education: Explorations in Evaluation.* Washington: American Council on Education, 1954.

Dressel, Paul L., and Nelson, Clarence H. *Questions and Problems in Science: Test Item Folio No. 1.* Princeton, N.J.: Educational Testing Service, 1956.

Dunkel, Harold B. *General Education in the Humanities.* Washington: American Council on Education, 1947.

Ebel, Robert L. "Procedures for the Analysis of Classroom Tests," *Educational and Psychological Measurement,* 14:352–63, Summer 1954.

Ford Foundation. *They Went to College Early,* Evaluation Report No. 2. New York: The Foundation.

Garrett, Henry E. *Statistics in Education and Psychology.* 4th ed.; New York: Longmans, Green & Co., 1953.

Gerberich, J. Raymond. *Specimen Objective Test Items: A Guide to Achievement Test Construction.* New York: Longmans, Green & Co., 1956.

Holzinger, Karl J. *Statistical Methods for Students in Education.* Boston: Ginn & Co., 1928.

Jacob, Philip E. *Changing Values in College.* New York: Harper & Bros., 1957.

Keller, Charles R. "Piercing the Sheepskin Curtain," *College Board Review,* No. 30 (Fall 1956), p. 1.

Levi, Albert William. *General Education in the Social Studies.* Washington: American Council on Education, 1948.

Lindquist, E. F. (ed.). *Educational Measurement.* Washington: American Council on Education, 1950.

————. *A First Course in Statistics.* Boston: Houghton Mifflin Co., 1942.

————. *Statistical Analysis in Educational Research.* Boston: Houghton Mifflin Co., 1940.

————. "The Use of Tests in the Accreditation of Military Experience and in the Educational Placement of War Veterans," *Educational Record,* 25: 357–76, October 1944.

Pace, C. Robert. *Growing Points in Educational Research.* Washington: American Educational Research Association, 1949.

————. *They Went to College.* Minneapolis: University of Minnesota, 1941.

Psychological Corporation. "Better Than Chance," *Test Service Bulletin,* No. 45. New York: The Corporation, March 1953.

————. "How Accurate Is a Test Score?" *Test Service Bulletin,* No. 50 New York: The Corporation, June 1956.

————. *Test Service Bulletin,* No. 39. New York: The Corporation, May 1950.

Smith, Eugene R.; Tyler, Ralph W.; and the Evaluation Staff. *Appraising and Recording Student Progress.* New York: McGraw-Hill Book Co., 1942.

Stuit, Dewey B., *et al. Predicting Success in Professional Schools.* Washington: American Council on Education, 1949.

University of Chicago, Office of the University Examiner. *Annual Reports of the National Registration Office for Independent Schools.* For information, write to Marjory Etnyre, Secretary, National Registration Office of the National Council of Independent Schools, Room 103, 5801 Ellis Ave., Chicago 37, Ill.

Walker, Helen M., and Lev, Joseph. *Statistical Inference.* New York: Henry Holt & Co., 1953.

Woman's College of the University of North Carolina. *The Alumnae News* (Greensboro, N.C.) April 1956, pp. 12 ff.

AMERICAN COUNCIL ON EDUCATION

ARTHUR S. ADAMS, *President*

The American Council on Education is a *council* of national educational associations; organizations having related interests; approved universities, colleges, teachers colleges, junior colleges, technological schools, and selected private secondary schools; state departments of education; city school systems and private school systems; selected educational departments of business and industrial companies; voluntary associations of higher education in the states; and large public libraries. It is a center of cooperation and coordination whose influence has been apparent in the shaping of American educational policies and the formation of educational practices during the past forty-one years.